Mind and Meditation Power

---

2 Books in 1:

Rewire Your Mind and Third Eye Chakra

[Joseph Brain]

Text Copyright © [Joseph Brain]
All rights reserved. No part of this guide may be reproduced in any form without permission in writing from the publisher except in the case of brief quotations embodied in critical articles or reviews.

Legal & Disclaimer

The information contained in this book and its contents is not designed to replace or take the place of any form of medical or professional advice; and is not meant to replace the need for independent medical, financial, legal or other professional advice or services, as may be required. The content and information in this book has been provided for educational and entertainment purposes only.

The content and information contained in this book has been compiled from sources deemed reliable, and it is accurate to the best of the Author's knowledge, information and belief. However, the Author cannot guarantee its accuracy and validity and cannot be held liable for any errors and/or omissions. Further, changes are periodically made to this book as and when needed. Where appropriate and/or necessary, you must consult a professional (including but not limited to your doctor, attorney, financial advisor or such other professional advisor) before using any of the suggested remedies, techniques, or information in this book.

Upon using the contents and information contained in this book, you agree to hold harmless the Author from and against any damages, costs, and expenses, including any legal fees potentially resulting from the application of any of the information provided by this book. This disclaimer applies to any loss, damages or injury caused by the use and application, whether directly or indirectly, of any advice or information presented, whether for breach of contract, tort, negligence, personal injury, criminal intent, or under any other cause of action.

You agree to accept all risks of using the information presented inside this book.

You agree that by continuing to read this book, where appropriate and/or necessary, you shall consult a professional (including but not limited to your doctor, attorney, or financial advisor or such other advisor as needed) before using any of the suggested remedies, techniques, or information in this book.

Table of Contents

REWIRE YOUR MIND 8

INTRODUCTION 9
CHAPTER 1 ANXIETY AND NEGATIVE SELF-TALK 14
Types of Negative Self-Talk 16
How to Overcome Social Anxiety 18
CHAPTER 2 MIND HACKING 24
What Exactly Is Mind Hacking? 24
Claim The "Admin Rights" 25
CHAPTER 3 SETTING A ROUTINE 27
CHAPTER 4 REMOVE STUMBLING BLOCKS 34
CHAPTER 5 MENTAL MODELS FOR CLEAR THINKING 37
CHAPTER 6 LIVE IN THE MOMENT 47
CHAPTER 7 HOW COGNITIVE BIASES CAN AFFECT DECISION-MAKING? 57
CHAPTER 8 CHANGING THE PARADIGM 71
CHAPTER 9 ACHIEVING QUALITY AND NATURAL SUSTAINABILITY 80
CHAPTER 10 SELF-WORTH 89
CHAPTER 11 MEDITATION 94
Further Benefits of Practice 95
Why Mindfulness and Meditation: Importance 96
However Continually Being "in A Hurry" Isn't Sound. 97
Meditation and Mindfulness Dangerous: The End Approach 98
Your Mind Is Your Greatest Power 98
Influence: The Power To subdue 99
The Powerful Source Within 100
Mind Power: Definition 100
Mind Power and Creativity 101
Accomplish Something You Love 102
CHAPTER 12 BE PREPARED WITHOUT OBSESSING 103
Planning vs. Worrying 103

Writing Your Worry Diary *105*
Threats of The Past *107*
Living in The Present *107*
How To Live Today *109*
CONCLUSION **112**

THIRD EYE CHAKRA **113**

INTRODUCTION **114**
Third Eye Chakra Color and Function *115*
Nature of Balanced Third Eye Chakra *116*
Blocked Third Eye Chakra Symptoms & Self-Examination *118*
How To Awaken and Align The Third Eye Chakra *120*
Secret Tips for Balancing The Third Eye Chakra *124*

CHAPTER 1 CHAKRA MEDITATION **128**
How Do Chakra Meditation Techniques Work? *128*
Make Each Cell in Your Body Stir and Celebrate! *129*
The Benefits of Meditation *129*
The Health Benefits of Energy Healing *131*
Chakra Meditation Music and Chakra Colors to Meditate *131*

CHAPTER 2 THE 7 CHAKRAS **133**
Solar Plexus Chakra (Manipura) *133*
Root Chakra (Mooladhara) *134*
Sacral Chakra (Swadhisthana) *135*
Heart Chakra (Anahata) *135*
Throat Chakra (Visuddha) *136*
Third Eye Chakra (Ajna) *137*
Crown Chakra (Sahasrara) *137*
How Chakras Work *138*

CHAPTER 3 IDENTIFYING BLOCKED CHAKRAS **145**
CHAPTER 4 THE PLANETS AND YOUR CHAKRAS **148**
Your Root Chakra *148*
Your Sacral Chakra *149*

Your Solar Plexus Chakra 151
Your Heart Chakra 152
Your Throat Chakra 153
Your Third Eye Chakra 155
Your Crown Chakra 156

CHAPTER 5 BALANCING AND HEALING THE CHAKRAS 159

CHAPTER 6 WAYS TO HEAL AND BALANCE THE CHAKRAS 167

Root Chakra Healing.. 167
Sacral Chakra Healing... 169
Solar Plexus Chakra Healing 171
Heart Chakra Healing.. 174
Throat Chakra Healing 176
Third Eye Chakra Healing 178
Crown Chakra Healing 181

CHAPTER 7 REIKI HEALING.. 183

CHAPTER 8 CHAKRAS YOGA 188

Yoga for Root Chakra.. 188
Crow Pose 188
Yoga for Sacral Chakra 189
Pelvic Lifts 189
Yoga for Solar Plexus 190
Front Platform... 190
Yoga For Heart Chakra... 191
Heart-Centering Meditation 191
Yoga for Throat Chakra 192
Camel 192
Yoga for Third Eye Chakra 192
Guru Pranam.. 192
Yoga for Crown Chakra 193
Guru Prasad.. 193
Malasana Yoga Pose 194
Uttanasana 195
Mountain Pose 195

Sun Salutations *195*
Anjaneyasana *195*
Warrior II *196*
Bridge Pose *196*
Wide-Legged Forward Fold *196*
Savasana *196*

CHAPTER 9 HEALING THE CHAKRA WITH COLORS **197**

CHAPTER 10 HEALING THE CHAKRA WITH SOUNDS **203**

CHAPTER 11 CRYSTAL HEALING **209**

CHAPTER 12 PERSONALITY ANALYSIS USING PSYCHOLOGICAL ASTROLOGY **220**

CHAPTER 13 QUESTIONS THAT ARISE ON THE HEALING PATH **225**
Root Chakra *225*
Sacral Chakra *226*
Solar Plexus Chakra *227*
Heart Chakra *227*
Throat Chakra *228*
Brow Chakra *229*
Whole Body, Mind, Spirit *230*

CHAPTER 14 SECRET TIPS FOR THIRD EYE CHAKRA **232**

CONCLUSION **242**

Rewire Your Mind

How To Declutter Your Brain and Carry Out A Mind Hacking Process, Remove All Bad Habits and Wrong Paradigms To Achieve A Positive Attitude for A Successful Life Lived On Your Terms

[Joseph Brain]

Introduction

The voice of my subconscious grew stronger over time, refusing to leave me alone. It didn't stop at answering questions anymore—sometimes it actually told me what to do, like saying I needed to pay closer attention to what I was looking at. It said I was missing the important things in life.

The life I'd been leading, it said, was a recipe for disaster. It said that everything I did was my own choice, that my future was formed by the thoughts I told myself and the decisions I made. For example, when I told myself I wasn't ever going to amount to anything, well, that's what would happen.

I didn't want to listen to this kind of talk. Life was what it was, I figured. I hadn't been born lucky, and I wouldn't be able to change a thing about it just by thinking differently. But my subconscious disagreed. It insisted that my subconscious mind was more powerful than I thought. It decided to show me a physical example of what it was talking about, and I was pleased to see it chose to do so while I was playing cards. When my subconscious was part of the game, it remembered every play. I started to win some pretty good money based on what it was telling me. But after a few weeks, it stopped helping me. I demanded to know why.

"Because winning at cards, making money like this—it's not the way to happiness."

"I don't know about that," I said, fuming. "I was feeling pretty happy. So why did you even bother to help me at all?"

"Because I wanted you to be aware of how powerful the subconscious can be."

I was not impressed, but its plan did work. By showing me the difference it made when I did or didn't use my subconscious, I saw that my mind had hidden strengths.

Some days, as I walked the city streets, my subconscious made me study the nice homes in the neighborhood. "This could be yours," it told me.

Just the thought made me laugh. "Never. I'm not that lucky."

"If you say so."

"You have to be born rich to live in a place like that."

"If you say so."

It started to repeat that phrase a lot, and it drove me crazy. But my subconscious seemed to be having a good time.

"What are you always so happy?" I asked.

"I'm having a great time," it replied. "You see, before your accident, all you ever did was say negative things about yourself and be self-destructive. I wanted to answer, but there was no way for you to hear what I was saying. Everything has changed now that you can hear me."

I was curious. "Are you ever negative? Because I never hear you get angry or frustrated."

"Think of me as you would think of nature. Nature always wants to be in a positive state. Negativity isn't part of that. See there?"

I looked where he was indicating. "Yeah, so?"

"That tree is growing out of a rock. It hardly has any soil beneath it. But it survives because it wants to grow, to be positive. On the other hand, if it was in your frame of mind and knew it didn't have any soil, it might just quit growing."

I studied the tree, really seeing it there for the first time. It really was amazing, seeing how it had clung to life despite the lack of soil. I started to think about the idea of positive thinking and wondered if the concept could help me.

"Of course," said my subconscious. "David, I'm like a master gardener, and you are the gardener. I can do almost anything you can imagine. People who have used their subconscious to the fullest have done what other people said was impossible. They sent people to the moon. They have led nations. All I really need is for you to believe in me and use me properly. David, the way you've been using me until now is like a gardener not taking care of his garden. Your plants are scattered all over the place, the weeds have taken over, and nothing is going to grow."

The image of my life as a neglected garden was so clear in my mind, I couldn't help but identify with it. I suddenly wanted it all to change. I wanted my garden to grow rich with green.

"What am I supposed to do?"

"Surrender to my advice. Follow what I have to teach you."

"And what is that?"

"I have unlimited potential," it said patiently. "I can help you gain more power than you could ever imagine. I know it's difficult to believe something like that, since I'm invisible. But think about this. When you look at successful people, then compare them to those who haven't achieved success, you can't see a physical difference—other than the material goods which might surround them. The difference is invisible, just like I am invisible. It seems strange right now, but it will all make sense if you allow yourself to accept it. If you direct your subconscious in the right direction, you can accomplish great results. Then again, if you direct your subconscious in the wrong direction, it can destroy you."

I could almost see it. But I was still so confused. "Who are you really? What is your purpose?"

"I worked with the Creator to help you grow from your one original cell and become what you are now. When the stove gets hot, I'm the one that takes your hand off the burner. If something is about to fly in your eye, I close that eye. I regulate your temperature, make sure your heart rate is appropriate, keep you breathing, and help in many other ways. I come up with brilliant answers if you ask the right questions. Actually, you're lucky to have found me. Many people go through their entire life without discovering the vast potential they have inside them."

The concept was mind-boggling. To have an invisible entity of some kind performing all these functions, keeping me safe and healthy, seemed unreal. And yet it had to be real, since I could hear it talking.

"What do you need from me?" I asked.

"I work best when you use your imagination. I will use all my abilities to help accomplish your goals, whether they are for good or bad. Just think: if no one used their imaginations, where would we be today? Throughout history, people have imagined incredible things and were ridiculed by others, but many years later we realize how incredible the discovery it was. The automobile, flying to the moon, the radio wave, the light bulb, these are all inventions someone imagined. The idea started with a seed planted in the subconscious, where it grew and gained a life of its own.

"Look at Einstein, for example. He used his imagination so well that it took fifty years for the rest of the world to invent the proper equipment so that we could measure and agree with some of his discoveries. Even then, there is still more to be discovered. Einstein said he owed the majority of his findings to his imagination, and scientists are still trying to discover what was so different about his brain that allowed him to think the way he did. Since imagination cannot be measured with proven data, and since it is invisible, they will probably never find the answer."

It seems strange to say this but, after a few weeks, I started really getting along with my subconscious. Our relationship was similar to how a dog always wants to serve its owner, with my subconscious helping me even when I didn't always pay attention to it. Even so, it took me a while to get used to having my subconscious as such an outspoken part of my life.

Chapter 1 Anxiety and Negative Self-Talk
It can be easy to talk about how much we hate ourselves! For some reason, it is easier to talk about the things that you don't like, rather than the things you do. Perhaps it is the way that we were raised, our current society, or a natural biological phenomenon.

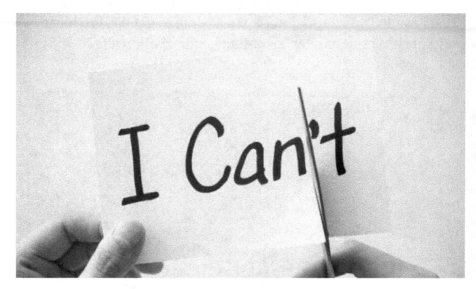

Self-deprecating jokes are the way to connect to others. When you can start to poke fun at yourself, then others might begin to relate and be able to do the same thing with themselves. There's still a line between poking fun at yourself and tearing apart your self-worth because of the flaws that you hate the most about yourself.

We can also start to relate to individuals that we might otherwise have differences with when we can gossip about other people. While you might like to discuss some harmless office gossip, make sure that this kind of negative talk doesn't go too far.

The problem with this kind of negative talk is that it is not giving us a positive perspective. We can start to lose sight of reality when we are only considering the worst aspects. If all you do is talk negatively about yourself and others, then this will weigh heavily on the way that you view yourself. When you are judgmental towards other people and make them feel bad for doing the things that they do, then you will speak this way to yourself.

Saying things like, "I'm not good enough," or "I don't deserve this," can be harmful in the long run. You will eventually believe these kinds of things as you are saying them. We start to say negative affirmations. This is a statement that affirms something. The more you tell yourself these affirmations, the more that you will fully believe them. That really changes your perspective on the world and yourself.

Turn these affirmations around and start to say positive things. It can feel weird at first. We're taught not to talk ourselves up too much because we don't want to seem too prideful. It's important not to be so egotistical and think that we're better than anyone, but that doesn't mean that we don't deserve to feel pride.

Before we discuss more methods for stress reduction in this specific area, let's make sure we're fully aware of what negative self-talk is.

Types of Negative Self-Talk

Some individuals will describe themselves as being self-aware. The issue is that many people think as though negative self-talk is being self-aware. Just because you are aware of your flaws does not mean that you are self-aware. It might make your awareness even worse when all you can focus on is the negative. To be self-aware is to be objective. You understand that you have some things that you need to work on, but you are also aware of the many benefits that you might add to the lives of others.

To have a high level of emotional intelligence, you also know that you can see the positive aspects of your life as well. Emotional intelligence is our ability to understand our emotions as well as the emotions of other people. Those with high emotional intelligence will usually have less stress in their lives because they are aware of where it came from and how to reduce it on their own.

It's good to be critical, but with things like saying, "we might have been able to do a little better," rather than, "we suck and shouldn't have even bothered in the first place." You should never talk to yourself in such negative ways because that's not productive. It's only going to make you feel worse and make it more challenging to change in a way you deserve.

Ask yourself in what area of negative self-talk you struggle with the most. Do you make yourself feel stupid and judge what you say? Do you hate what you see in the mirror and continuously speak poorly about yourself? Whatever area of negative self-talk you participate in most, recognize it so you can understand why.

Where did this come from? The voice that is telling you negative things likely didn't just start on its own. It is a combination of the things that we have gathered from the world throughout our lives.

There are pressures from society. Growing up in certain schools, you might have had people judge or bully you that warped the way you think about yourself.

Our parents can create these voices. Even the well-intentioned parents might play a role in the way that we view our self-worth.

A lot of the time, it is we who suffer the most and causes that perspective. The more you judge yourself, the more you will judge other people and vice versa. No one is perfect, everyone has flaws, and we all deserve to be given a chance and treated with kindness.

What This Does to Your Perception

When you can't stop thinking negatively and talking to yourself in such harsh ways, it can lead to a close-mind about yourself, and about the world in general. You will warp the way that you view everything in life, and this can eventually become somewhat toxic.

You will start to believe everything you say. The more you let that negative voice take the mic and lead how you think, the more that you will begin to silence the positive view that provides you with reason.

This can stress you out. You'll want to continually do better when you tell yourself over and over that you can't do anything right. You'll feel as though you are never good enough, and this pressure to be perfect can add a ton of stress on your life.

You will create incredibly high standards for yourself that are almost impossible to reach. You will become disappointed when you can't reach these goals and think that there is something wrong with you. This will make you feel even worse, sending you into a toxic cycle that induces high levels of stress.

You will make yourself feel worse and worse after you've done something rather than building yourself up and getting to a place where you feel better about yourself. You won't be able to accomplish anything if you are making yourself feel terrible all the time.

Eventually, it can lead to feelings of depression and anxiety. You will be too depressed to do anything, and anxiety can keep you trapped as well. Start to reverse these thoughts you have about yourself to live a more stress-free life.

How to Overcome Social Anxiety

If you hate yourself and never give yourself the chance to feel better, this can end up leading to social anxiety. You might start to become afraid to leave your house, go to parties, and even hang out with your closest friends and family members all because of the intense social anxiety that you are feeling.

You might struggle with social anxiety if you fear going out in public, talking to other people, or just generally being in the presence of other people. It can be hard to schedule a doctor's appointment on the phone or even respond to a comment on social media when you have crippling social anxiety.

Social anxiety can keep us from doing the things that we love the most. You might want to see a band live but choose to skip the show because you fear others that will be there. Maybe you want to go grocery shopping for a nice dinner but instead, choose to order takeout again because it means not having to be in public around others.

When you always put yourself down, then you might get to a point where you don't want to be around others at all. This can make you feel completely isolated and alone, another emotion that can add even more stress to whatever feelings might have already been there.

Remember, first and foremost, that everyone is going to be more focused on themselves than you are of them. When you are afraid of something like a hissing cat or a spider, these things seem scary. However, they are only doing this because they are scared. Spiders might look like creepy little bugs, but they're more frightened of you than you are of them. Remember the same can be said about other people. While you might be feeling anxious, maybe not in your best outfit for a part, remember that everyone else that goes to this party is likely going to be anxious about the way that they dressed as well.

Don't assume control over other people's happiness. You are not in charge of making sure everyone has a good time, and a small joke that you make isn't going to ruin the party. Social anxiety can make us feel as though we are the ones that have to make sure everyone's emotions are in check, but remember, only the individual has the power over the way that they feel.

Always question your thoughts. Look at where they came from and work through them at the root. How would you treat someone else that was in the same situation? What advice would you give to a friend? Never say anything to yourself that you wouldn't feel comfortable saying out loud to a friend. Next time you look in the mirror and think, "I'm so ugly," ask yourself, would you call your friend, "so ugly?" Hopefully not. So then why is it OK to say this to yourself?

Start to expose yourself to social settings in small amounts. Maybe at first, it will just be ordering something crazy off the menu at a coffee shop. Next, you might try to go to a group setting. Maybe eventually you are able to throw your party. Whatever you have to do, start small and work your way up the social ladder.

Afterward, remember that you have already lived through the experience, and there is no going back. Don't sit there and ruminate over what happened. The moment has passed, and you can move onto bigger and better things.

Ask questions, and get to know more about others. This is a good way to practice being more social. If you are afraid to talk in a conversation, then ask. Think of anything you want to know about them, and actively listen to what they're saying when they speak. This alone can help you feel more comfortable and keep you grounded in the present.

Stop Worrying About What Other People Think

Some people worry because they want to please everyone and take care of virtually everything. They strive for perfection in a multitude of tasks. Trying to dabble in more tasks than you are capable of handling is a sure-shot worry trigger. Your inability to deal with multiple tasks leads to nervousness and frustration.

It is crucial to remind yourself and others that there are only so many important tasks you can handle without making a mess of it. It is alright to ask others to pitch in when it comes to sharing responsibility.

You can delegate tasks or enlist the help of co-workers. This doesn't mean you do not care about work or people. It simply means you are prioritizing your work and life to make way for lesser worrying and more living. You are only taking on those tasks that you can do justice to rather than everything that clutters your mind with worry.

Set a self limit to the time spent on assisting others. Design limits based on the type of caring that causes worry. Remember, worrying doesn't fix anything. Worries should not be allowed to go past a particular point, and enforce your limit whatever it takes.

The objective is to live the best quality of life as long as you can. You are not going to drop dead if you do not eat that bowl of fruit one day or indulge in your favorite dessert. It is alright to let go sometimes. Permit yourself occasional slacking or periodic indulgences.

Worry begins with a potentially nagging thought. Maybe, a small and harmless trigger unleashes it. The tiny nagging thought creates a few more thoughts. Before you even realize what is happening, the mental storm starts brewing. It makes you think irrationally, unrealistically and in highly exaggerated proportions. You drain your physical, psychological and mental energy.

The mind is now filled with complete chaos. Worrying and negative thinking can have a profound impact on the way you think, act, feel and behave. It prevents you from leading a fulfilled and happy life. How then does one stop worrying? What are some of the most powerful techniques to lead a worry-free life? How can you stop worrying and start living? Here are some solid and action oriented tips to help you break free from the worry cycle.

When you actually do something you have been worrying about for long, you nip it forever. Many times, our worries are centered on our ability to pull off something successfully. There is an inherent fear of not being able to do something.

Pick something you have always wanted to do or do even better or start doing again. Give it your best. Remember – you do not lose anything by trying. You were as it refraining from doing it, which means you had already given up. Folks who are successful and happy are not much different from you. The only difference is they do not allow their worries, fears and negative thoughts to prevent their positive actions. Pursue something you have always wanted to pursue after weighing all options without the fear of failing. It can be about launching a start-up you have always wanted to build or learning martial arts or traveling alone. Once you start doing something you have been thinking negatively about and do just fine, it can do a world of good to your confidence.

If you do worry about what you can't control, you're going to instantly increase your anxiety by exposing yourself to a factor that's bound to sting sooner or later. You would keep yourself stagnant and immobile, unproductive.

Leave it at that and let the negative opinion be their problem, not yours. Carry yourself with high esteem and walk away from unconstructive criticisms that are coming from a place of insecurities.

You need to move on and focus on the positive, focus on your values and find comfort in knowing that you act in a way that's aligned with your belief system. And feel safe with the realization that you know where you are going, and it is where you want to go. Embrace yourself and let go of everything else.

Stopping The Self-Hate

Remember that your thoughts aren't always necessarily true. Just because you think the same thing over and over about yourself doesn't mean that this is something that you should believe. We all have different things about ourselves that we don't like, but you must remember your biggest insecurities aren't things that you have to tear yourself up over.

Question where these thoughts come from and rephrase them in a way that makes you feel comfortable saying them to someone else. If you aren't comfortable sharing these thoughts with others, then they might be too negative.

Accept the things that have already happened. You can't go back in the past, so forgive yourself. The mistakes you might have made already occurred, so there is no point in trying to change things or wish they hadn't happened. You don't have to let this define your present and future life, so make sure that you let go of the things that are out of your control.

Allow yourself to be imperfect. You wouldn't expect perfection from those that you are closest with right? So why do you think that you have to be perfect?

Look for ways to improve in smaller, healthier habits rather than expecting to become a different person overnight. Practice with positive affirmations. Always tell yourself, "I can do this," and "I am worth it."

Sometimes, looking at the worst-case-scenario will help you understand that it isn't so bad after all. If you make an embarrassing joke at the party, is that the worst-case scenario? Absolutely not! So, don't be afraid to do things like this. It's better to share a few things, maybe one of them being embarrassing, rather than staying completely isolated all night.

Remember that it is going to be a training process. It took years to build that negative voice in your head, so it is going to take a while to get rid of it as well.

Chapter 2 Mind Hacking

What Exactly Is Mind Hacking?

The dictionary shows two different meanings for the term *hack*. The first definition explains that hacking means to write computer programs for enjoyment. Another definition puts it differently: "to gain access to a computer illegally." But we are not going to do something illegal hereby privately stealing the information from someone else's mind. This book is not about hypnotizing somebody else and getting the results you want from that person (though who wouldn't want to control the thinking of their boss and get a hefty salary hike?).

We are accessing and trying to control that data in our own mind—nothing illegal here.

Also, another thing to notice is that the term *hack* has recently entered the general usage with a new non-technological sense, meaning "solution" or "work around" as in the usage "life hack."

But here is the best definition of hacking for the purposes of this book:

This book intends to follow the approach suggested in the above definition, which means we will analyze the "source code" of the mind, imagining (based on what we see elsewhere) how best we can make this code to do something different, then reprogramming the code by stretching our own capabilities in order to change our lives for the better.

You are reading this book because you want to learn the secrets of the complex programming of your mind with the objective to use the maximum potential of your brain for attaining success in your life. You are not here to just understand the bare minimum concept of the mind necessary to operate at a reasonable level because chances are that you are already using your mind's bare minimum capacity for working. You are here to learn the deeper secrets of your mind, and that requires claiming and exercising special rights to get inside your mind, as you will learn now.

Claim The "Admin Rights"

Assume you work in an office environment or any other community-like structure, where many people work together using computers connected through a common server. You might have experienced, while installing some program or software on your computer, seeing a message on your screen stating that you don't have the administration rights to change the computer's pre-existing setting by some new software. Your computer requires you to take permission from the controller of computer's network before you install any third-party software on the computer. You are not granted the rights to change the software settings of the computer because it might adversely affect the whole network, if you inadvertently install some malicious software.

In this case, you have got only the "user" rights, which means you can use the computer only for the limited purposes of doing your work, as determined by the organization or community you work with. But the controller of the network has "admin rights," meaning he or she can make any changes, install or remove any programs or software, or do anything at the computer network level. Therefore, unless you get the admin rights, you can't make any changes in your system.

Similarly, to hack your mind, you need to empower yourself with the *admin* rights; after all, you are going to reprogram your software, install new applications, remove the bugs out of your mind, and anything and everything significant to get the best out of the computer of your mind.

When you keep on working the way you have always worked, based on what your family, school, work environment, or society has taught you to be, you have given yourself the "user" rights of your brain. You are using only the pre-installed system and software, and therefore you are able to do only the limited amount of work and innocently assume that you are delivering your best. It's only when you dare to think beyond what is programmed in your head for ages, that you decide to take charge of your mind and eventually your own world. It's only when you are convinced about the malleability of your brain, about the plastic nature of your mind that you think of transforming yourself into a different and changed human being.

But remember, you have to be all in; lukewarm will not do. If you are super curious to know the complex layers of your brain, if you are prepared to do the experiments with your own mind, if you are ready to put in what it takes to harness the power of your mind, then welcome, you have already got a hold of the admin rights for your mind's software. And no, you don't need to seek permission from someone else.

OK, since you have already assumed the admin rights available to you, let's start the process of hacking your mind to do everything that is needed: uninstalling the old programming, installing the new software, and coding new programs using our imagination to get the best out of us.

Before you can bring in new material, you need to get rid of the obsolete and non-usable items to make space for the novel things.

Chapter 3 Setting A Routine

When we were growing up, many of us used to be reminded the time to go to rest, and the time to wake up, when we need to do our homework, the time to shower, eat dinner and play with our friends.

However, this doesn't happen when we become adults. Many adults don't have a specific schedule for their day. In fact, most have no clue of what they are going to do once they wake up because they haven't decided to create a schedule to follow. Therefore, this makes many grown-ups to become stressed, overwhelmed, anxious and falling short of their true abilities.

The way to solve this is to create a routine timetable that works well for each one, and one that allows us to become productive, controlled, and the best person we can be.

I once saw a daily routine as monotonous and restrictive, which I'm sure is an opinion many shares. They live their life, thinking they are free somehow, in a wild and fantastic way. Rather, it has come to my attention that the way to liberty, productivity, joy is so we can realize our real potential is to develop and adhere to a routine. Hence, with a certain routine, we would all be better off.

If we follow a routine every day, the need to make choices every day is lessened. It allows us to understand precisely what duties we have to perform daily without too much contemplation. We understand what happens next without too much thought when we're done with one assignment. Activities are listed, which leads to greater efficiency.

When we design a routine thoroughly, our activities must be scheduled every morning, and our precious time must be allocated. A daily routine offers our life framework and reasoning. It offers the basis for our life and events every day. We soon become acquainted with what we need to do daily and become comfortable. It allows us to experience the flow of current.

We spend free time on planning, decision-making, and training by following a routine. Our timetable has been predefined and enables us to use our time effectively. Repetitiveness is the key to healthy practices. It promotes the development of healthy behaviors, motivating us to do the same tasks whenever designing a private routine that works for us. Just as every morning, we adhere to a routine that enables us to promote practices which correspond to our objectives and ambitions.

While our routine enables us to build good practices to make full use of our potential, also, it makes us eliminate bad habits that don't work well for us. By repetition, we can slowly substitute our poor habits with excellent ones. This enables us to first and foremost achieve our goals when we design and follow through on our tasks. We understand the importance of completing our tasks, and the sense of accomplishment when we get to cross something off the list is quite rewarding.

The value of developing a certain routine obliges us to prioritize and to decide what we care about. We already understand what to do and what to do rather than take these choices every day, because we have scheduled them closely. After searching for my soul and looking closely at it, for instance, I decided to make sure I was conscientious and healthy so that I incorporated meditation and training into my routine.

Whenever a collection of tasks and activities becomes a routine, it cuts down the odds that we will postpone doing them. It becomes part of us to the point where we can do it subconsciously.

Repetition builds momentum, making it easier to continue when you do the same stuff repeatedly. This is why it's simpler to go to the gym; the more often you do it. The passage of time is an important factor in ensuring achievement and helping to create that momentum following a routine.

It enables to create trust and provides us with a feeling of enormous fulfillment when we adhere to and follow a routine. That gives us the fuel to carry on and take advantage of our routine. And one of the primary reasons why it is hard for individuals to alter their life for better is lack of self-confidence.

It can assist us in saving cash if we follow a routine and do the same stuff again and again. For example, every morning, juicing of fruit and vegetables is part of my routine. I can buy my fruits and vegetable in huge quantities, saving me cash because I understand that I'm going to follow this routine religiously. The same goes for much more, such as the price of membership in the long-term gym.

Certain things will always be beyond our control in our lives, and we must acknowledge that. However, we can regulate so much, particularly if we follow a routine. It cuts down on the pressure when we design and stick to a routine because we do not need to figure out what needs to happen next.

Rarely if ever, are our objectives and ambitions accomplished at once. Successful individuals achieve their objectives by repeatedly doing the same stuff. A sportsman gets excellent at his game if he continues to practice daily. An artist constantly repeats his craft.

One of the safest ways of ensuring your achievement is to develop and stick with a routine consistent with your objectives.

It's an excellent method to monitor progress. We can then create changes and return to our private routines while trusting that we're back on the correct track.

Be aware that it's all right if you decide to pursue your routine on weekends alone, or in case you have a different routine on Monday, Wednesday, and Friday. It's also completely all right to elect to do nothing. You have closely considered this and are aware of your decisions.

The main thing here is that you need to consider it and remain aware of your decisions exhaustively. A routine is a deliberate decision to live your life in a certain way. It is one of the secrets to success and good fortune. Each of us has specific wishes, needs, objectives, and resources.

Therefore, after thoroughly choosing what we want to accomplish in our life, it is essential that we create our own routines. It certainly is worth the attempt to reap the benefits. Today is a new day, and it is never too late to begin your routine.

"We are what we repeatedly do. Excellence, then, is not an act, but a habit."- Aristotle

Because I didn't want to live my life according to the regulations other people set for me, I struggled against developing healthy practices and routines. Besides, keeping a routine was hard work.

It turns out that it's much more emotionally exhausting to have no routine or structure whatsoever.

By avoiding to do what I knew would help me. For example, meditating, creating a list of gratitude and exercising, I took away the energy that these kinds of beneficial operations produce from my body and mind. Indoors and out, I felt tired. My dreams and objectives just fell away, leading to isolation and a feeling of helplessness.

Now, I am more motivated and passionate, which makes it possible for me to fulfill my goals. I have enough mental and bodily electricity to make my days interesting, even days when it is tough for me. I find happiness and more comfort with the excellent and depth of my life.

One of the changes I had to make for this to happen was to shift my view about routines. When I'm suffering through a depressive episode, I tend to rely heavily on making a schedule and sticking to it.

I admit it though: creating productive habits isn't effortless.

Here is something that you need to recall: what works for someone else doesn't mean that it will work for you. That is why it is important to choose tasks that go well with you. Go for tasks that allow you to become the better version of yourself, and maintain those tasks.

Don't be scared to keep your feet in fresh water and learn how it works for you. If they leave you feeling rejuvenated, then you need to hold to them. If they don't continue trying new ones until you find the right one, the secret is to build normal and steady patterns daily, that will push you to where you want in life, allowing you to take advantage of every stage as possible.

A daily hobby makes you attain laser-like attention from the time you rise in the morning to the time you close your eyes. Below are some ways to consider.

Be positive: Start the day with motivation. It could be anything, from positive affirmations to repeating one task you're determined to do that day. This kicks off your day with the right kind of mindset. Don't overwhelm yourself with a list of tasks right as you wake up; center on yourself first.

The purpose of this is to send a command from your conscious thinking to your subconscious mind. Your unconscious idea has to agree with what you say to it, and it will do anything to change the instructions into a reality.

Make sure your day-by-day to-do list is relatively short so that it is something that you can complete and not overwhelming. An important technique to ensure that your list is easy is to apply the Post-It-Note. The measurements of a Post-It-Note are great because the size limit will make you to entirely record the most critical thing that you have to do every day.

Although each of the above tips is meant to help you move forward, sometimes, you only need to give yourself a break. Breaks will prevent you from getting bored and losing your concentration. At the same time, breaks will boost the function of your brain. It will force you to reevaluate what you are working on, making sure that you are moving in the right direction.

Subdividing your day into smaller tasks ensures that you remain at the top of your game.

While all of these tips are supposed to help you forge ahead, on occasion you just need to step again and give your thinking a break.

If you spend a lot of time doing just one thing, it can make you lose your interest and focus. And if you are working on a task you hate doing; it makes it less difficult because you will only be doing a little of it.

Spend your time working on what you want by optimizing the output in the least time. The way you value your time and use it is what is important. Try to review your day and figure out how you can divide it up into blocks of time, where you also have time for recreation.

It is fine to become flexible when it comes to building new habits. In other words, be specific on what you are searching for, but maintain the flexibility to work inside your lifestyle so your habits can stick.

No two days are ever the same. Our mental energy might be prepared to complete tasks one day and totally depleted the next. So, if you can't do it all at once, that's okay. Don't feel guilty or like you're not productive enough. The American Psychological Association suggests that to enhance our success, we should focus on one goal at a time.

Chapter 4 Remove Stumbling Blocks

Take the biography of any successful leader or philanthropist, you will learn a great deal about self-discipline from them. What problems they faced, how they overcame them with persistence and confidence, what hurdles they crossed, what barriers they broke, etc. All of this is a testament of how crucial it is to learn self-discipline and practice it in all phases of our lives.

If you dream of becoming as successful as them, you need to work on yourself. Now that we already have an execution plan, learned the role persistence plays, and acknowledged our weaknesses, the next step involves getting rid of any distractions that interrupt your focus. Distractions can lead you astray, prohibit you to face your fears and make facing challenges impossible.

Therefore, when trying to learn self-discipline, it is pivotal that we stay away from any distracting elements and try our best to remove them from our lives.

5 Super Distracting Blocks To Avoid
What things are considered distractions? Let's take a look below.

1. Giving Into Temptations

We know by now that temptations are nothing but means of distractions. Be it eating a tub of Ben & Jerry's, watching a freshly-released episode of your favorite TV series, missing out on your workout routine in the morning so that you can sleep in a little longer, or wasting time scooping around from one article to another instead of finishing your assignment are all forms of distractions that are rooted from temptations.

All of these examples take your focus away from the actual goal – building self-discipline. Self-discipline requires that you perform one thing over and over again without complaints, boredom, or guilt until it becomes a habit.

Beating temptations is hard but with fulfilling rewards, it becomes a possibility. However, failing to resist them only paves way to demotivation and failure. Even if you don't feel like it, the key is to stick to whatever goal you wish to achieve so that one day, when you look back, you don't have any regrets.

2. Losing Heart Too Soon

Giving up too soon is one of the primary reasons that hinder one's path to achieving self-discipline. Things won't happen for you overnight. You won't lose weight, you won't control your temper, you won't stop lying, and you won't quit smoking. All of these require time and persistence. It is natural to feel frustrated when you don't see things happen the way you thought they would. There are a hundred reasons why things go wrong but only one that leads to complete failure – giving up too quickly.

Even if your self-esteem hits a new low, you mustn't stop fighting and continue to move forward. Try setting smaller and practical goals with a realistic timeline. Next, just stick to it no matter what.

3. Stress

Many psychologists believe that stress is indirectly proportional to self-discipline. How many times have you made the right choice when stressed out or anxious? Not many. Whenever we are stressed, it feels like our brain has stopped working. And to be clear, it isn't always mental stress that gets in the way of things. Sometimes, even physical stress causes problems. Acute or chronic stress are two types of physical stress in which the normal functioning of the body is modified. The symptoms may include headaches, dizziness, panic attacks, etc. It can be episodic or permanent. Episodic stress may be caused by things as simple as tough work schedules, a big presentation, and fights with a partner. Whereas, examples of permanent or chronic stress include loss of a loved one, traumatic childhood, depression or loneliness, etc.

Whatever it is, it needs to be managed when trying to learn self-discipline in life. Some mental conditioning activities include counselling, yoga, or medications – things we shall discuss in detail in the next chapter.

4. Procrastination

Procrastination is another hindrance in becoming self-disciplined. Procrastination is the practice of delaying things with lame excuses. We all do it, intentionally and sometimes unintentionally. It is the evil root cause of wasting time till the eleventh hour and then doing things in a hasty manner. You must realize that there is no time like now and if you aren't making the most of it and utilizing the available resources, you are going to fail in achieving your goals. The key is to work on today so that your tomorrows are successful and fulfilling.

5. False Hope Syndrome

False hope syndrome is synonymous to having too high of expectations. When expectations are too unrealistic and you fail to accomplish your desired goals, you are bound to feel bad and want to give up. Like stated several times, things need time, energy, and stability. When there is a wide gap between the expectations you have and the expectations you should have, problems will propagate automatically.

Chapter 5 Mental Models for Clear Thinking

Every day, our minds are filled with information from everything that is happening around us. As a result, we are left with the challenge of clearing our minds to pave the way for effective thinking. Allowing too much to flow in and out of our minds prevents us from thinking right. The use of mental models can be useful in helping us to think clearly. Most people use these models every day, but they might not realize that they are doing it. When thinking of how you can best relate with your friends and relatives, you are using a mental model. When pondering on how to budget for your monthly expenses, you're also using it.

Any framework used to help you in grasping something easily is perceived as a mental model. Practically, these models can be identified as the apps present in your mind. With the help of each app you have stored in your mind, you can make the right decisions. Also, the more apps you have, the easier it will be to solve the problems in your life. Why? This is because you have a wide array of tools that suit different kinds of problems that you might be going through.

This chapter takes on a specific angle on how mental models can help you think clearly. With the advancement in technology, there is a wide array of devices that can be used to gain access to information. The advent of the internet, for example, has made information available to us whenever we need it. Unfortunately, this flooding of information has been more of a distraction to most individuals out there. Accordingly, mental models are more important than ever before. So, we must learn how they can be used to bring about clarity in how we think.

How To Think Clearly

Clear thinking is not as easy as you might think. It is a challenge that most people have to go through more so when they have to deal with other stressful issues. Your ability to think can also be affected when you're feeling tired and overwhelmed. There are several basic things that you can do to help yourself think clearly.

Check Your Attitude

Your ability to think clearly will largely depend on your desires. Often, you will find it easy to sit down and think of the strategies that you can adopt to achieve your goals. Of course, this is dependent on if you have goals. When you don't want to achieve something, it is also easy to think of all the things that you can do not to accomplish this. Therefore, to think clearly, it is imperative to be honest about your goals and ambitions. Is this something that you really want in your life? Ideally, developing the right attitude will be helpful toward bringing clarity in the goals that you wish to attain.

Use Your Passion

There is a good reason why successful people will always advise you to follow your passion. The reality is that you have never heard them tell you to follow your emotions. Your passion toward a particular goal will help you to overcome any challenges associated with it. Passion drains away all the negative thoughts that could deter you from thinking clearly about the task ahead. Conversely, emotions will do just the opposite. Allowing your emotions to get the best of you will only make you feel overwhelmed about what you should do. Usually, you will find yourself focusing more on the obstacles that you must go through. Therefore, to think clearly, it is advisable to use passion to keep your emotions in check.

Use Negative Thinking

It might sound controversial that you should use negative thinking to help you. It is possible. Remember, we are talking about finding the right frameworks to help you understand something better. So it is worthwhile to consider how negative thinking can help clear your mind.

Believe it or not, there is a positive power in negative thinking. When striving to achieve goals, most people will embrace the idea of thinking positively. Certainly, thinking positively works in many ways. It gives your mind a chance to focus your energy on what you can do to ensure you accomplish set goals. Interestingly, negative thinking can help you understand the main reasons why you might not accomplish a particular goal. Therefore, looking at this from a positive perspective, you can take advantage of your negative thinking to bring about positivity.

For instance, consider a scenario where you aspire to work in a competitive industry. If you want to work in one of the best firms in the industry, reflect on some of the reasons why you might not be hired. Some of the reasons that you might list here include your lack of skills in that particular field and your lack of experience. Using these "why not," you can convert them into "how to." Therefore, to effectively land on a good job, you will have to take relevant courses and thereafter gain experience by taking on different jobs. So, if you can tap into the positive power of negative thinking, you can help set your mind to focus on what you want.

Use Cool Logic

Achieving a clear focus you need on what you want to achieve might be easy in the short run. Most people find it easy to concentrate for a few weeks or months before losing track of what they are doing. Therefore, as part of ensuring that you maintain a clear focus on what you desire, you should use a cool logic. How does this work? Cool logic relates to the idea of concentrating on the issue at hand. You should not allow anything else to distract you. For example, if you are working on a project, your mind should concentrate on the project and nothing else. Normally, it is easy to get distracted and allow your ego to control how you think. In this case, you will be withdrawn to think about how you are better than others in doing a particular task. As a result, instead of focusing on the task at hand, you will pay too much attention to competing with your colleagues. Ultimately, this will have a negative impact on the outcome of the project.

Challenge Your Preferences

Several presumptive beliefs could affect the clarity of your thoughts. The ideas that you have developed in your mind about a particular issue can deter you from thinking about anything else. A good number of people will want to settle for the most expensive wines simply because they believe in the notion that the price of the bottle determines how the wine tastes. However, this might not be true if you engage in a blind taste test. You might come across something that you will like. The point here is that you should challenge your preferences by trying something that you have never done before. You will be surprised that you could make informed decisions to the least of your expectations.

Think About Thinking

The aspect of being aware of your thought processes is termed as metacognition. For you to think clearly, you should be aware of how you are thinking. Therefore, you shouldn't allow your thoughts to flow freely without being aware of them. Instead, it is imperative that you plan and assess how you are thinking. The advantage gained through metacognition is that you will enrich your learning experience. For instance, your self-awareness will drive you to think clearly about how to accomplish a particular task.

Ideal Mental Models for Clear Thinking

You will find it easier to make smart decisions even when faced with difficult situations. However, you can improve on this by learning to use some of the best mental models on clear thinking. Combining the tips with the models that will be detailed here will ensure that you have varying perspectives of looking at any situation that you are faced with. Just to remind you, the more mental models you know, the easier it will be for you to make smart choices.

First Principles Thinking

Some problems appear too complex for us to solve. Without a doubt, this is a dilemma that most people go through in their lives. Well, you shouldn't be stuck when faced with such circumstances because you can apply mental models. An ideal mental model to use here would be the first principles of thinking. This model comes highly recommended when dealing with challenging situations. The best part is that this framework will push you to think for yourself.

The first principles thinking has been there for several years, but it recently became popular in 2002 after Elon Musk stressed on the importance of using it. This framework focuses on the idea that one should think like a scientist. The reason for taking this direction is because scientists don't use assumptions. Their conclusions are often made after facts have been proven.

Theoretically, first principles thinking will require an individual to think critically about a certain situation until they are left with the truths that define the problem they are facing. This is to mean that you shouldn't make decisions like other people. You should mull over thinking deeper. The easiest way of grasping the meaning of this principle is that when faced with a problem, the first thing that you should do is to deconstruct. After that, focus on reconstructing.

The first step of deconstructing requires that you ask yourself intelligent questions regarding your situation or problem at hand. Additionally, you should have a deep understanding of frameworks from distinct disciplines. It is crucial that you get more information about varying forms of mental models. Your knowledge is required to guarantee that you can look at your problem from varying perspectives.

Your next move will be to bring together the pieces that you had broken down in the first step. Again, for you to effectively reconstruct, you have to practice how to do it. You could have an idea of how to do something. However, a standalone idea cannot help you to make good decisions. You need to combine several ideas to make valid conclusions. Practicing this more often will strengthen your mental muscles. Eventually, you will improve your thinking skills and end up making sound decisions.

Jeff Bezos used the first principles thinking at the time he established Amazon in 1995. He had two principles that would guide his business to thrive. First, his goal was to focus on the long-term. Secondly, his mission was to focus on the customer instead of the competition. Certainly, with these guiding principles, Bezos managed to drive his company to blossom and become a global market leader.

Thought Experiment

The thought experiment mental model can help you think clearly by solving difficult problems. The thought experiment encourages speculation. What's more, it forces people to alter their paradigms. Instead of reasoning like other people, thought experiment model pushes you out of your comfort zone. As a result, it forces you to ask yourself rhetorical questions that are complex. Through this style of thinking, it unveils the things that you don't know and some of which you know.

The advantage gained in using the thought experiment is that it encourages innovative ideas by pushing you beyond your thinking boundaries. Therefore, you will not be limited to the things that you already know. One major challenge with this mental model is that it appears impractical. Nevertheless, scholars believe that it can be used theoretically.

BATNA

BATNA is the acronym for Best Alternative To a Negotiated Agreement. This mental model can help you during negotiations. Normally, there are instances when negotiations reach a deadlock. This is a situation whereby parties cannot agree on a particular issue. In such cases, there should be an ideal alternative since parties negotiating cannot agree.

It is worth noting that BATNA should be taken into consideration even before engaging in negotiations. Before entering into negotiations with any individual, you should be aware of your BATNA. The benefit that you gain here is that:

- It gives you the best alternative in case you fail to agree.
- It gives you an upper hand during negotiation since you will have negotiation power.
- It helps you dictate your reservation point. This is the lowest price that you can accept in the deal.

Therefore, knowing your BATNA will help you to think clearly when negotiating with people. Going into negotiations without BATNA will only influence you to settle for anything just to close the deal. This is not a smart way of making decisions.

Compounding Knowledge

Compounding knowledge is a mental model rooted in the economic concept of compounding interest. The framework is not only applicable in your investments, but it can also be applied to your business, relationships and knowledge.

People are always on the verge of consuming information. What they fail to realize is that most of them consume expiring information. This is something that Warren Buffett strives to steer away from. Instead of focusing on consuming information that is not important, Buffett focuses on equipping himself with the knowledge that would help him manage his companies successfully. The idea here is to learn something new that would bring about a positive change in what you do.

Gaining and gathering information from time to time will undeniably lead to compounding benefits. Learning something today and combining it with something else that you learn on the following day will make you a better person. Filling your mind with expiring information that is of less importance is easy, but the reality is that it will not help you in days or months to come.

So, how do you tell that you are consuming expiring information? Information that is marketed to you is not as useful as you might think. Also, if you find that the information lacks meaning and that you can easily consume it, then chances are that the information is not credible. In addition, you will soon realize that it will be irrelevant after a short while. Take, for instance, the habit of watching the news and keeping yourself updated on what is going on around you. Doing this only fills your mind with expiring information. Why don't you spend this time garnering knowledge about things that will help you in years to come?

Of course, we are not saying that we should copy the likes of Warren Buffett, but it is important that we acknowledge how these models have helped people to succeed in their lives. Accordingly, there is a lot that we can learn from how they choose to use these models.

Occam's Razor

Occam's Razor is a mental model that is attributed to William of Ockham. He did not introduce the term, but his style of reasoning inspired people to come up with the heuristic. The simplest way of comprehending this concept is that the simplest solution to a particular problem is regarded as correct.

We cannot deny the fact that we always strive to simplify our lives. Everybody does. However, we find ourselves complicating how we live and how we deal with our problems. Interestingly, some billionaires astound us with the way they choose to live their lives. Mark Zuckerberg is a good example. It is not uncommon to see him in a gray T-shirt. If you can recall, Steve Jobs also wore his black turtleneck for almost all occasions. This raises eyebrows, right? Indeed, these folks can afford fancy outfits, but they choose to wear similar outfits most of the time.

Using Occam's Razor philosophy, simplicity is the key to success. The idea of wearing similar clothes every day as evidenced by some billionaires is a way of saving themselves time. Without a doubt, knowing that you will wear a gray T-shirt every day can help you save time. Moreover, it can save you brain power that you can use in making informed decisions. The point here is that you should not allow trivial things to distract you from focusing on what is important.

Clearing your mind to help you make the right decisions is not an easy feat. One important fact about mental models is that they complement each other. This means that for one mental model to be effective, you have to apply other models in your decision-making. In addition, you should embrace the idea of gaining more knowledge about a particular matter. Don't just limit yourself to one or two models.

Chapter 6 Live in The Moment

Meditation is a major key for many life problems, it can help you calm down and learn to control your thinking. Numerous studies and research articles concluded that mediation can help cope with stress, anxiety, and depression. It teaches you to let go of your feelings and control your thoughts. It is the key to free yourself from the inner chaos within your mind. How it works is that it removes the toxic thoughts and negative things that your mind observed during the day by enhancing what is useful and the knowledge that you have stored inside your inner mind. You are becoming more aware of the things that you are learning and observing, as well as your own subconscious. It holds the great power to purify and bring balance to your mind. If you are struggling to fall asleep during the night or suffering from remembering certain things, then meditation is the cure you've been waiting for. It can help calm your thoughts and learn to control them so whenever you go to bed, you will know how exactly you can fall asleep without having your mind jumping to all possible conclusions about your life. Here are a few key steps to follow while meditating.

Choose the Right Time and Environment

When people first start off meditating, they often fall asleep after a few minutes. You must be aware that you are meditating, so it is recommended that you do it in the morning when your mind is fully awake and ready for the brand new day ahead of you. You need a peaceful environment with no interruptions, so put your phone on silent or lock your doors. It is completely fine if you are able to hear some outside noises, but try not to get too distracted.

Get Comfortable and Set a Time Limit

It is important that your body relaxes as so does your mind. Sit down somewhere comfortable or lay down, but make sure you won't be able to fall asleep by removing a pillow or putting an extra pillow under your head. Start off with around 5-10 minutes a day and as you continue, raise your time by about another five minutes.

Notice Your Breath

When you are settled in, close your eyes and relax. Notice the way your chest falls up and down as you are inhaling and exhaling. Clear any thoughts or worries that might be clouding your mind and focus on what is happening right now and how you are letting go of the negativity. It is perfectly normal that your mind starts to wander to other places and other thoughts pop out in your head, like where should you go for lunch today. When you realize your mind has wandered off, bring it back to your breathing. Repeat until your time is up. Your goal is to make sure your mind is blank and as quiet as possible without any thought interruptions. As you practice more throughout the week, you will become more experienced in it and will be able to do it for longer.

You can also meditate with music, no not the kind with lyrics otherwise you will find yourself singing along inside your head.

The best music for meditation is the 432 Hz tunes, which is the harmonic intonation of nature. It has healing properties for the brain; it will fill you in with a sense of peace and balance. The certain beats and sounds inside the tunes are often connected to the brain and the way it functions. For example, the sound of bells activates the brain cells or the sound of water activates the neurotransmitters. This helps the mind relax even more and it could help stop your mind from wandering off if you are just aware that you are listening to the tunes. It is also possible to grant you access to the rest of the brain, the other parts that you don't use throughout your life.

Pay attention to the patterns and your reactions to certain situations without giving it a thought, you have to become aware of the things that you are doing in order to stop them. For example, imagine yourself always being mean to your younger brother, and you find yourself snapping at him often without even thinking about picking a fight. This is a sign of a pattern; your subconscious mind is so used to fighting back and protecting yourself from what is in store in the future that you find yourself fighting when it's not needed. So take a deep breath and calm yourself, you have already become aware of your condition which will prove it easier to stop and re-program. Next time the situation occurs, make a mental self-note to prevent yourself from exploding with anger, tell yourself to calm down and that this is not the proper way to solve things. That way your subconscious will realize that you are starting to change routes in your habits and will have no choice but to follow along.

Visualization is an important key to success and achievement. It can help reprogram your mind and help you attract the things you want in life. Visualizing can help push your fears and worries aside and open up a new feeling of hope to the possibilities around you. You can even do it after you meditated and your mind is relaxed and free of any negative emotions. All you have to do is use your power of imagination, imagine yourself in the situations that you only dream of. If it's something as small as receiving a promotion or as big as buying that car you've always wanted. You can put emotions and feelings of excitement when you finally receive what you were longing for. This is a strong element when it comes to attracting things into your life and it connects to changing your mindset. You see it in your head, think about it constantly and act as if you already have it, then, sure enough, you will attract it into your life. For example, if you want to lose some weight, you imagine yourself and how happy you would be when your goal is accomplished, this promotes motivation because you will then want it even more than before and it pushes you to try and accomplish your goal.

After meditation, you can start to visualize your goals and dreams. When you are under deep relaxation, it becomes easier for you to change your brain patterns and reprogram yourself through something that is called self-hypnosis, which when you are hypnotizing yourself. You have a certain brain frequency in you right now because you are awake and your mind is focused. Your brainwaves move from Beta(14 Hz to 30 Hz) to Alpha (8 Hz to 14 Hz) to Theta (4 Hz to 8 Hz) and lastly to Delta (0.5 Hz to 4 Hz). Delta would be the last state which usually occurs when you are in a deep sleeping state. Theta is when you become sleepy, Alpha is relaxed but alert and Beta which you are now, fully awake and alert of all your surroundings. It becomes so much easier to reprogram your mind and subconscious through Alpha and Theta. If you begin to imagine and visualize your goals and beliefs with repetition a couple of times, it will be easier to get rid of any doubts and will become much easier to attract those things into your life. You can do it after meditation when your body is already fully relaxed, just don't get up yet. All you have to do after is just visualize your objective. If you choose to not meditate but you want to jump straight into visualizing in the Alpha and Theta state, then lay down and relax your body, each part one by one by slowly letting go of the tension you have there. When you finished, just visualize your objective for a few minutes and try not to doze off! It can be hard at first try but if you practice continuously you will surely get better at it.

If you are having trouble visualizing, then create a vision board. A vision board is just a place where all your dreams and desires are written on. You can make a collage of pictures of the house you want, the job you are aiming for and the clothes you want to be able to afford. It can be anything you want it to be, add a quote for inspiration and every time you look back on those pictures, imagine yourself in them, for example, walking through the house that you wish to have or walking into the office of your job. Look at the quote and read it to yourself, every time it will pop up in your head or you look back at it, you will remember your goals. You can also attract a certain person or beloved into your life, write down their qualities in terms of personality or looks and think about them often, then sooner or later they will walk through the door.

Don't listen to other people if they tell you they failed. Failure is the key to success, if someone just decides to give up then what kind of success would they achieve if they keep on giving up after every hardship that stumbles upon their life. You must be willing to change for the better, you can't have doubts in your head about it because your mind is always listening, if you constantly have to tell yourself 'don't worry, this will work' when in reality you are not really sure and you are just trying to trick yourself into believing it, then it will take longer. Know that everyone is different, although we have the same brain structure, our subconscious mind is different because not everyone experienced the same thing as you did. This makes some people more loyal and strong-minded than others. If everything was easy and training your subconscious was as easy as ABC then everyone would be successful, there won't is much of an opportunity to prove people wrong or satisfaction for achieving the desired outcome.

Make a gratitude list, which is a list of things that you are thankful for. You need to learn to live in the present and not in the future. Don't focus on what you will have in the future and the things that will make you happy then but instead look around and thank whoever or whatever is in your life. Thank the universe and life for providing you with basic things like eyes to be reading this or a pen to write with. This will open your subconscious to more positive feelings and will help to put a barrier against the negative ones. Make a to-do list on the next page of your gratitude list to keep up with your tasks if you keep on forgetting certain steps to reprogram your subconscious. Eventually, this will turn into a habit and you will no longer need a list to keep track because your mind will be doing this subconsciously.

Let go of the word 'how'. How will I achieve something so big? How is that even possible? Focus on yourself and nothing more. Your body and mind have been caring for you ever since you were born and now it's your turn to repay them by maintaining a healthy lifestyle and any doubts in your head. The mind is the most powerful place in the universe, it is compared to be much more complicated and stronger than a computer. So start asking yourself what you want and not how you going to achieve it. It's like an online store, shop for whatever you want, the possibilities are countless, add it to your shopping cart, pay for the delivery and you will have it at your doorstep in no time. The universe knows 'how' everything will happen and when the time is right, it will tell you.

Have a jar of affirmations, not only it can help you change your mindset but also train your subconscious mind. Write on a piece of paper your good qualities, things you like about yourself and things that want to become. For example, if you lack self-confidence, write 'I am confident'. Write around 10-20 each on a small piece of paper, fold it and put it inside a jar. Every day, pick out a new piece of paper to boost your self-esteem and self-appreciation. Remember what the paper says about yourself, and believe it. If it says 'I am confident' then act confidently today, it is your ticket to do anything you want. Think of it as your future self-telling you what you have become, read it, understand it and believe it.

Your body is not the only one that needs exercising, because your mind needs it too. Learn to exercise your mind by solving puzzles or playing mind games. The mind loves to learn something new every single day and what better way than to exercise it at the same time. Expand your knowledge through countless games and quizzes online, try to learn something new every single day, a new vocabulary word or something as big as solving the Rubik's cube. Everything then is stored inside your subconscious mind, allowing it to grow further.

Finally, you must rewrite yourself as a person. Plan your entire day and don't waste any second of it. If you don't have them already, make a few healthy daily habits. It is important to stay consistent throughout your journey of success. Make a new habit, stick to it and repeat it, that way your mind will thank you. Take a fifteen-minute walk in the morning to your local coffee place before you go to work or make a habit of listening to motivational podcasts at least a few times a week. Little things like that can really change your world. Rewrite your own story, because you hold the pen to your destiny. If something is bothering you, then seek help or change it. It is never selfish to seek and want plenty of things, it just shows that you have a lot of space to grow to become the best version of yourself that you can be.

How do you tell if this is actually working? The steps you followed above for weeks but you can't seem to achieve your goals. Once it happens, you will know if your subconscious mind started to change. You will find yourself to be happier and less focused on your current problems. You will develop a sense of confidence and your mental state will feel so much stronger. Realize that the universe is all in your favor, face risks and challenges because life is short and you will have that opportunity to grow and you can't accomplish your dreams if you just follow the exact same boring road when you can stumble upon shortcuts. You are always one decision away from a totally different life, only you can shape your own destiny and future.

First remember that it is not easy to change your subconscious mind, it has been around for way longer than you came into the realization of the world around you. Do not get discouraged if it doesn't work straight away. It's almost as hard as stopping smoking or drinking, except you have many of those habits all around you. The mind likes to play tricks on us, it might try to convince you that you can't do it and change it because it has its own self-awareness, so you must prove it wrong. Say you read this book, you might have come to a realization that you clearly understand what it says, however, your subconscious mind did not because you are not making a habit of reading this book over and over again. The baby steps to change yourself and accomplish your dreams is what your subconscious mind will come to realize as a pattern if you make it into a habit of doing these things. It is hard to change yourself, turn yourself into a completely different person, and not everyone is mentally strong enough to do this. But reading this book is already a huge step towards success, you are processing this information into your head and making a side note to continue in following your dreams.

Let's quickly summarize the process of re-programing and expanding your subconscious mind. The first step is to change your environment, you want to be happy then bring happiness into your life. You could also adopt a puppy, although they may seem like a hassle at first, it is scientifically proven that they bring happiness into your life, relieve you of stress and loneliness, and make you leave the house to walk them more often, which is good for your body. Stay healthy to reward your body and your mind for doing a good job. Meditate daily, make a habit of training your brain to keep your thoughts in check, this will surely prove itself useful in other aspects of your life. Visualize your goals and desires, the inner mind is responsible for your imagination and to access your subconscious mind, all you have to do is imagine fulfilling your goals and desires. If you have trouble with visualizing, then just use a vision board instead. Make sure to pay attention to any patterns and habits that you like to do subconsciously. Don't let other people tell you what to do and fill your head with unnecessary doubts. It is you who chooses what to believe. Make a gratitude list. You can make a jar full of affirmations, and read one to yourself every day or you can just recite affirmations in your head without having to write them down. Rewrite your own story, you get to decide your future and nothing else so make sure to think about what you want in life and how you are planning on achieving it. Exercise your mind, learn new things.

What do you do when you achieve that correct mindset or the perfect subconscious mind? You can change anything in your outside world if it's a job you want to change or start a relationship. It's simple, all you have to do is focus on the area of your life that you want to improve. If it's a job opportunity that you want to attract then focus on it, tell yourself that a new job opening will become available to you, pray or meditate to it every day. The universe is like a catalog, you can get anything you want, all you have to do is set the right intention. Your subconscious mind will be used by now when you wish and visualize the things you want in life so, in order for them to come true, you must believe that they are already on their way. You also must put in a little effort, for example, go in search of a new job opportunity, don't just sit there and wait for it to magically appear because the world doesn't work that way. You have to physically do something in order to get to your goal. It is right in front of you, all you have to do is put some effort to reach out and grab it. So, all you have to do is wait and visualize the desire that you want, put some effort and it will find itself to you.

Remember to be reaching for the stars for the right reasons. If your success somehow gives harm to those around you, the universe can always take away what you earned and worked for. The law of Karma, which states that what you give will come back to you. If you do good deeds then the universe will find its way to reward you, however, if you stray from the path of light, then misfortune will follow you. You must remember not to become corrupted with the power of your mind, and do think for the good of yourself and others around you. Make sure to spread happiness and love to everyone around you, help out a friend who is in need of guidance or if you see someone suffering, make sure to step in and intervene. Good things come to those who do good.

Chapter 7 How Cognitive Biases Can Affect Decision-Making?

There is a wide range of complexity within the world. It is not possible to process all the information available within the surroundings. So, you will have to follow mental shortcuts for making a decision instantly and effectively. Cognitive biases based on the processing of information are statistical and you can fix them easily with the new information. Emotional biases are problematic to adjust or change as they are structured considering feelings and attitudes involving consciousness or unconsciousness. There are many reasons which can cause cognitive biases. The mental shortcuts or heuristics play an important role to cause cognitive bias within a person. Some cognitive biases such as confirmation bias, Halo effect, availability bias, attentional bias, self-serving bias, functional fixedness bias, anchoring bias, misinformation bias and so on can distort an individual's thinking ability.

Confirmation Bias

When an individual decides by accepting information or reference which supports his or her existing belief within matter or events, it is considered as confirmation bias. Generally, it involves statistical errors as it works through information which people gather and interpret. Mostly, it allows people to make poor decisions. It usually blinds people when they observe anything. It impacts an individual in what way he or she has gathered information. But it also affects the interpretation and recalling of information. For example, when a person believes in a mater or event, he or she will search information to establish his or her belief. He or she will also explain new stories by following a way to uphold his or her existing ideas. He or she will also try to remind the detail within a way strengthening these attitudes.

Halo Effects

When you think about a person and try to get information about his or her overall impression, it is considered a type of cognitive bias which influences your way of thinking procedure. This type of cognitive bias is named as halo effects. Usually, it influences your evaluation of a person's character including a specific trait. For example, when you think about a celebrity as an attractive, loving, and successful person, halo effects will influence you to explain his or her character as intelligent, funny, and kind. In your daily life, there are some situations that involve halo effects. These situations are when you are trying to find out something which is attractive or which is related to your workplace or school or healthcare or the way of your responses due to due to a marketing campaign.

The Dunning Kruger Effect

Generally, when people are less smart and incompetent to do work, they think that they are enough smart and skilled persons for doing any work. The reason is that they are affected by the influence of the Dunning Kruger Effect. Dunning and Kruger found this type of cognitive bias when they had made tests for students within the field of grammar, humor, and logic. The result showed that the students were extremely overestimated their score who scored minimum marks. On the other hand, the students had done well score who made slightly underestimation about their score. When a person makes overestimation about their skill or performance, it helps to increase their confidence. But it affects their performance by creating a bad score as they cannot identify what they can do better or what level of performance is considered a good standard. If they can identify the reason for their failure, they will be open-minded to make criticism and set about to fix them.

Self-Serving Bias

A self-serving bias explains the common habit of an individual to take credit for positive outcomes or effects. But he or she blames others or outside factors for negative effects or outcomes. The primary cause for self-serving biases is based on a defense mechanism that enhances the self-esteem of an individual. When a student appears in the examination without taking proper preparation of his or her studies, he or she blames on others and circumstances for being unsuccessful within the examination. He or she blames such as the teacher didn't teach him or her with care or environment of the classroom was not appropriate for giving the examination.

Ambiguity Bias

Ambiguity effect explains that the people generally avoid the option with hinder information as it may make your choice risky. People like to choose the potion which is available with known probability to achieve a favorable outcome. Ambiguity bias represents that people don't like uncertainty and always try to avoid it at any cost. Ambiguity bias can affect your marketing procedure. When potential customers are influenced by ambiguity bias, they feel the fear of the unknown. They will choose your competitors when they will notice the product or services which are known to them.

Availability Heuristic

Your brain helps to apply strategies and to utilize methods when you want to get a solution for any issue. A heuristic is a term that explains mental shortcuts for making your choice. You follow heuristic to make your choice or judgment. Eventually, these shortcuts play an important role in deciding within a faster and easier process. The availability of heuristic is one of the mental shortcuts frequently utilized by the brain to find out a solution for an issue. It judges the possibilities of events how easily and instantly examples can reach your brain.

The Curse of Knowledge and Hind Sight Bias

The curse of knowledge happens when an individual processes information by following imperfect ways. When you are influenced by the curse of knowledge and hindsight bias, you spend specifically the major time for observation of things from your perspective. You forget or ignore that the level of other people's knowledge and perspective is different. As a result of this, you become a failure to completely fit from the anchor of your own perspective. You will feel difficulties to account for the information that thought, views and beliefs are different from you.

Projection Bias

Projection bias influences people to think that other people will feel, think, behave, and believe in a similar way which they do. You will assume that the way of thinking or doing anything is usual. So, the other people will react within a similar manner as you do. You will overestimate the way of other people thinking or opinion for being similar to your opinion. As a result of this, you will make a decision that will fulfill your recent emotional stat or wish without targeting your goal for the long-term. Projection bias is also called an empathy gap. You will be influenced by projection bias when your present emotional state biases your prediction. Projection can influence the people to make the planning for the future such as making the plan for retirement savings.

Conformity Bias

Conformity bias influences you to behave within a pro-social manner rather than utilizing your judgment. When early men lead their life as hunter-gatherers, they work as a team and collect their essential items to survive. If anyone is departed from the group, he or she will suffer from less food, housing, and protection. On the other hand, if he or she stays within a team, he or she will achieve reproductive success easily. Sometimes, if you are influenced by conformity bias, you will state the incorrect answer according to your group, even though the correct is known to you. Conformity bias influences people for wishful thinking which is a type of self-deception like false optimism. Self-deception can be compared with a drug. It can numb your unfavorable reality or turn you to a tough matter regarding thinking or collection of evidence.

Optimism Bias

If you are affected by optimism bias, you will get involved within mistaken belief which explains that your chances to suffer from misfortune is less and your chance to attain success in life is more than those of your peers. It will lead you to be overly optimistic and as a result of this, you will make the wrong decision regarding important matters within your life such as decision for a health check-up or decision for financial investment and so on. It will influence you to make a poor decision which may result in a dreadful situation. For example, people might forget to use a seatbelt, to skip yearly health check-up or forget to use sunscreen before going outside and so on. When you are influenced by optimism bias, you will think that you are luckier than others and you will be surely in a safe position while others may be in problematic situations.

Attentional Bias

Sometimes, when you make an important decision, you consider the things which you like to consider. But there are also some important things which you overlook. These types of activities are explained as the influence of attentional bias. It can lead you to make bad or improper choices. You will neglect the other aspects of an event or situation as you are concentrating on some selective things. When people are affected by the symptoms of depression, they also suffer from some chronic diseases such as diabetes, hypertension, and arthritis. Depression is also a common factor of attentional bias. Moreover, depression is also involved in the absence of position attentional bias. Attentional bias acts as negative stimuli for making a decision. For example, when you think about to purchase a new car, you will pay attention to the look of the exterior and interior parts of the car rather than the safety of the car and the mileage of the car. This type of behavior of any person is the effect of attentional bias.

Authority Bias

Authority bias represents the tendency of human character to weigh the suggestion of an authority figure more important. They are also more flexible to be convinced or influenced by an authority figure. For example, the different marketing companies use advertisements to influence the customers by authority bias. When a celebrity endorses an advertisement for a particular brand, you usually rely on that brand without doing any judgment. In 1961, Stanley Milgram made the experiment of Milgram obedience based on authority bias. He was a professor at Yale University and his subject was psychology. His experiment explains in what way the authority bias influences people even within their daily life. He also suggests that people should have to understand the influence of authority bias which they generally underestimate.

Loss-Aversion Bias

The key idea of less-aversion bias was explained by Amos Tversky and Daniel Kahneman in the year of 1992. According to loss-aversion bias, the pain of losses is twice as powerful when you will compare it to equivalent gains. It is also one of the essential foundations of Prospect Theory. Prospect Theory explains how people make their choice among different options of prospective and also how people estimate the perceived income of these different options. For example, you have ordered lots of food for your family in a restaurant as you think that you and your family will enjoy all the food completely. But, when you will feel that all the food will not be possible to eat, you will be influenced by loss-aversion bias. If you want to avoid the influence of loss-aversion bias, you should maintain self-awareness and you should keep understanding the context when you will decide for the next time.

The Sun Cost Fallacy

There are several reasons when people are affected by many possible psychological traps. After planning for something, when you will realize after some time that your plan will not serve properly, you will try to correct your plan for not getting the return according to your expectations. This situation is explained as the sun cost fallacy.

The Negativity Bias

When people give more importance to negative experience than a positive experience psychologically, it represents the influence of negative bias. The effects of negative bias are stronger than positive emotions. For example, you may have made appreciations your loved one for many times. But there will cause a great impact on your relationship when you make a single insult to him or her. It is no matter how many times you have appreciated him or her. But, one serious negative comment or insult can cause breaking within your relationship. There are mainly four types of negative biases and these are negative potency, negative dominance, negative gradient, and negative differentiation. Generally, people keep negative remark within their mind than positive. It is an example of negative potency.

Functional Fixedness

When people observe within a specific portion of an object and work on it ignoring the remaining part of the object, it is termed as functional fixedness. It doesn't allow people to the full range of an object and also acts on it. As a result of this, people are not always able to think about the right or alternative solution for an issue. Functional fixedness is a type of cognitive bias which restricts a person's ability for viewing with a wide range to make a judgment or a decision. It can create troubles in both creativity and problem-solving areas. It reduces creativity because it resists people to think outside of the box. They continuously return to their one-way track.

Actor/Observer Bias

Actor/Observer bias influences people to be more effective within the circumstances to result in a negative outcome. For example, actor/observer bias influences the people for blaming another person when they get to a negative result for their actions. Generally, actor-observer influences to create a problematic situation. It frequently causes a situation of arguments and misfortune. Actor/observer bias explains the tendency of people to attentively their actions to external causes. But they attribute other's activities as an internal cause. For example, when you have a high level of cholesterol, you consider that it is an issue related to genetics. But, when you consider the reason for others' high levels of cholesterol, you will explain it due to insufficient exercise and poor diet.

Framing Bias

Framing bias influences your brain to make a decision considering in what way the information is presented. It influences the decision-makers and purchase within the marketing policy. Framing bias encourages a participant negatively while options are framed involving risks. It also utilized by the advertiser to influence the customer's view.

Framing bias affects human psychology and it is a type of cognitive biases. When framing bias influences people, they show their reaction unknowingly on any matter or event which are conveyed to them. One of the most common effects of the framing bias is observed within the behavior of older people. They generally try to present something positive as they want to avoid the risk of anything. Framing bias can influence you while you will decide for financial or health policies.

The Backfire Effect

The backfire effect influences people by resisting them to accept evidence which is contradictory to their beliefs. People support their preexisting beliefs when they are influenced by the backfire effect. It influences people so strongly that they deny for considering probabilities which they have thought in the wrong way. For example, when the researched voting preference about the candidate shows a negative result, he or she is influenced by the backfire effect to increase his or her support for that political candidate. When people want to encounter information that doesn't support their beliefs and their feelings for being threatened causes different types of negative emotions. They will try to establish that political person's specific ideas and identity.

The Decline Bias or Declinism

Usually, people give more importance to negative emotions than positive emotions. It has been researched that decline in attention, memory, working memory, execution of function and inhibition are common in human beings with the increase of age. Decreased functioning of the brain causes due to age. As a result of this, the ability for understanding context and maintenance of information becomes less and it affects the performance of an aged person.

Bandwagon Bias

Sometimes, people adopt style, behavior or attitude as many people are doing that. This type of activity is termed as a bandwagon effect. It is a type of cognitive bias which plays an important role in making errors within the thinking of a decision or a judgment. For example, a person starts to wear a specific style of clothing as he or she notices others to adopt a similar fashion or style. A person is highly affected by bandwagon bias when he or she wants to be perfect. When people observe that most of the people are doing something, they think that they will have to do it otherwise they will be isolated from others. Moreover, when people are influenced by bandwagon bias regarding health issues or political decisions, it can cause damage seriously the consequences.

Strategic Misrepresentation

Sometimes, a company starts a large-scale project involving a high level of overruns cost and overestimation budget. But they fail to continue their business due to insufficient managerial skills, poor location, and strategic misrepresentation. Strategic misrepresentation is systematic distortion or misstatement of facts to respond to incentives with the budget procedure. It is an expected response to the structural form of incentive within the budgetary game. It can word considering some specific consequences. It is used for advocating budget.

In-Group Bias

When people are positive and helpful towards the members within his or her group, it is termed as in-group bias. Generally, it is present within the different fields of reality such as religious beliefs, political ideology, and geographic identities. For example, a member of a political party supports and helps the other members with his or her group. On the other hand, they show their negative attitude to the other political parties. But, when the supporters of any political party change their group over time, they start to support that political party and the members related to the new group. In-group bias is generally available within the different social groups, on different dimensions, in different settings, and in many various cultures. The members of in-group bias have more positive behavior than the members of out-group members. In-group causes due to the structure of the natural environment. When an individual is threatened or worried about his or her self-concept, he or she is influenced by in-group bias.

Fundamental Attribution Error

Fundamental attribution error is also termed as correspondence bias. It influences people to overemphasize dispositional or pre-reason-based description for conducts notices in others while others give importance to the situational description. People are influenced by cognitive bias to think that a person's activities depend on personal characteristic rather than the elements of the social and natural environment which affect the person. In 1977, Jones and Harris Ross had argued that the conceptual bedrock within the psychology is made by the fundamental attribution error. Generally, we observe anyone's conduct according to their internal motivation and responsibility. The perceptual features are pressed within their character that could be insufficient information regarding the behavior to the observer.

Anchoring Bias

Anchoring bias influences people when trying to make their decision using an anchor or initial point. It has been researched that people generally rely strongly on the information which they learn first. Sometimes, people go to purchase anything, they make an estimation of their purchasing considering the initial value of anything. Anchoring bias generally influences the people when they are failed to evaluate something. Sometimes, people determine the quality of a product considering the price of that object. For example, people assume that the product is excellent, high quality, long-lasting and stylish when the product is expensive. Anchoring bias influences people when they make their decision for the money-saving aspect. It influences them by tempting and convincing them for purchasing more units even there is no need to purchase them.

Misinformation Effect

The misinformation effect explains how the memories easily get influenced and create a doubtful memory. This type of cognitive bias is related to the eyewitness memories which are utilized to detect the criminal offense. Sometimes, questions are placed to an eyewitness contain misleading information which can distort the person's memory of that crime or event. When an individual will be influenced by the misinformation effect, he or she will not be able to rehearse actively the details of a given happening after encoding. Due to the expansion of the period between the real-event presentation and post-event information, the usual thing is that an individual will include misinformation with their final report. Moreover, if you provide more time to study the real event, it will reduce the chances of the influence of the misinformation effect.

Status Quo Bias

Generally, people like to stay the way which they follow. If there is a need to make any changes the people get scared of those changes. This condition is explained as the influence of status quo bias. It is a type of cognitive bias to refer to an event of preference which is related to one's environment and/or circumstance remains as it already exists. In 1988, Zeckhauser and Samuelson introduced the term status quo bias firstly and they had described this type of bias using several decision-making experiments. It has been described using several psychological principles that involve loss aversion, cognitive dissonance, sunk costs, and much more exposure. These principles are explained as a logical reason to choose status quo bias. The status quo bias influences people when they like things to remain in the same condition by avoiding doing anything or by sticking with the same decision which they have made before.

Pro-Innovation Bias

The pro-innovation bias represents a type of belief that a change should be chosen by everyone within the society when there is no need to make its alteration. The pro-innovation bias explains any circumstances where you will give attention specifically to the good in something and ignore the bad. For example, you observe a high range of registrations for tools to focus as new social media. But, the rate of using the tools is low. Performance focused institutions have specifically induced the aspirants by using pre-innovation bias to exaggerate their success which is essential to build a bright career.

The Forer Effect

The Forer effect is a type of cognitive bias and it influences an individual's belief with a wide range of pseudoscientific practices such as palm reading, astrology, fortune teller and so on. The Forer effect is utilized to encourage people to think that a service, product, or advertising campaign has been made significantly for a selected group of specific people. The Forer effect is also known as the Barnum Effect. In psychology, the Barnum Effect has been utilized in ways. One way involves in creation of feedback for an individual who has been selected for psychological experiments. He or she will read the feedback and will rely on it as a created personality for him or her. The other way of the Barnum Effect involves a study of an individual's personality by using a computer. The personality ratings provided by the computer generate feedback about an individual's personality. Generally, it works positively when the statements of feedback are positive.

False Consensus Effect

False consensus effect is a type of cognitive bias and it influences people to think that their concepts and values are normal and so the majority of the people will agree with the same opinion. Sometimes you may try to understand whether the people within your family and friends who have similarities with you. The reasons for occurring false consensus effects are related to the same consequences. When there are more similarities between you and your family members and friends for having similar beliefs and behavior, people are influenced by the false consensus effects. When you believe that the other people are thinking by following the same way which you like, you will be motivated or self-esteemed with the influence of the false consensus effect. Moreover, when you are the most familiar with your own beliefs and attitude, you will be influenced by the false consensus effect. You will try to find out the people who have the same attitude as you.

> "All of us show bias when it comes to what information we take in. We typically focus on anything that agrees with the outcome we want." – Noreena Hertz

Chapter 8 Changing The Paradigm

"You can't change the fruit without changing the roots." – Stephen Covey, author of the best-selling book The 7 Habits Of Highly Effective People

Consider the mango tree. Its fruit is one of the world's most favorite because whether ripe or raw, mangoes are such a delicious treat. Year in and year out, you can expect a mango tree to yield mangoes. Unless it dies by tree-cutting or extreme and extended drought, it will yield mangoes regardless of the weather condition or goings on in the environment.

What would you make of trying to make mango trees yield, say, bananas? Crazy, right? What about the person who's doing everything he or she can to get bananas out of the mango tree? Crazy too, right? Honestly, they can succeed in doing so albeit for a very short while. How?

They can hang a bunch of bananas on the branches of the mango tree and pick the bananas from there, can't they? They can, in their minds, believe that the mango tree yielded bananas. But it won't last long. They'll eventually see how cumbersome it is to hang bananas there before picking them to eat – they can just eat the bananas directly. They'll realize the absurdity that it's futile to force the mango tree to bear bananas every year.

LIFE FRUITS

Your life is just like the mango tree. It will yield fruit according to the root, which is a mango tree. Trying to "act" differently from your existing roots may yield some degree of success but that won't last long and your life will revert back to what it is rooted on. The fruit doesn't fall far from the tree.

If you want bananas, plant banana trees. If you want apples, sow apple seeds in the soil so that when it grows to maturity, it will yield apples year in and year out effortlessly. If you want to live a consistently successful life, plant trees or roots of success. There can be no other way.

The soil in which your trees are rooted in is your subconscious mind. To enjoy fruits of success continuously and naturally, you need to plant success trees. Just like natural or physical trees, it will take consistent care and time for the trees to bear fruit.

In practical terms, how do you plant success trees in the soil that's your subconscious mind? By using your conscious mind.

THE CONSCIOUS-SUBCONSCIOUS CONNECTION

To a great extent, you are very much aware and can control what you say. To an ever-greater extent, you pretty much have control over where you want to physically go, e.g., the bathroom, the supermarket or the basketball court.

Consider this, can you control your heart – command it to stop or beat slower? You can't right? Your subconscious mind is what regulates it. Consider your sweat. Can you, by sheer will, make yourself sweat, say even in cold weather? That's also a function of your subconscious.

That doesn't mean, however, that you can't direct or influence your subconscious mind. You can. In the same manner that you can't make the soil yield mangoes on its own no matter how fertile it is, you can plant a mango tree that will yield your desired fruit.

Just like a calculator, the subconscious mind is automatic but is dependent on inputs from your conscious mind or the environment. In the classic self-help book called Psycho-Cybernetics, Dr. Maxwell Maltz called the subconscious mind a ServoMechanism, which is a mechanism that automatically seeks a goal and will not stop until it's achieved. He compared it to a heat-seeking missile, i.e., all it needs is a target and it will, by its own, seek that target and won't stop until it succeeds.

According to Dr. Maltz, this is the reason why no amount of will power in the world will result in lasting change or success. Will power is on a conscious level but since the subconscious is more powerful, merely acting on the conscious won't work. The subconscious needs to be reprogrammed for lasting success.

Bob Proctor explains how to reprogram the subconscious through this diagram:

The results you're getting in your life right now are the effects of your body's actions. And most of these actions, believe it or not, are highly influenced by the subconscious mind through feelings. And guess what? The subconscious mind is highly influenced by the conscious mind. That being said, you can consciously influence how you feel.

Although you can't directly control the subconscious mind, there's good news: it is open to all suggestions. According to Bob Proctor, it can't reject suggestions. When we were babies, we were open to all suggestions and acceptance of these manifest when we became toddlers. This is how some children, without formal language training, grow up to be tri or multi-lingual. Just being exposed to an environment where many different languages are spoken, they're able to learn how to speak multiple languages. That's how open and powerful the subconscious mind is.

To better understand this, consider the stick man analogy used by Bob Proctor in his seminars:

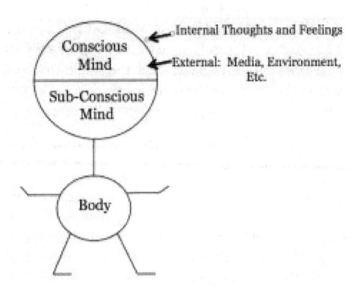

The head houses the brain, which controls the whole body. The mind is a function of the brain. Every suggestion that enters the subconscious mind comes from the conscious mind, be it our own thoughts or external suggestions from media, other people or the environment that pass through the gateway that's the conscious mind.

The subconscious mind, based on the inputs provided by the conscious, generates vibrations (also known as feelings) to the rest of the body, which acts on such vibrations and propels you to the target or goal that was downloaded to the subconscious.

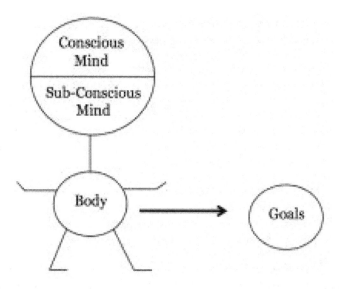

I'd want to use my nephew as another example of how open the subconscious mind is. Back when he was 5 years old, we were shocked to hear him say something that was considered Rated X or for adults only. We wondered how on earth did he learn to say those things when his parents didn't speak that way at home. Where did he get that? From mainstream media, particularly television and radio. Why? Because at that age, his conscious mind wasn't well developed yet, which meant all those things he saw and heard through media went straight to his subconscious mind unfiltered.

As an adult, you may think that your subconscious mind is no longer as open to all suggestions but the truth is, it still is. It's just that you don't realize how powerful – or weak, as the case may be – your conscious mind is as the gatekeeper of your subconscious. Whatever you purposefully impart by suggestion or passively plant by laxity to and in your subconscious mind, they're easily accepted by the latter. No ifs and buts. The problem then lies in your ability to consciously control your conscious mind.

That's why as you grow, so should our ability to control your conscious mind. When you exercise control over your conscious mind, you can successfully filter what is passed on to your subconscious mind. If you use your conscious mind to purposefully plant seeds of success, i.e., success thoughts, in the soil of your sub-conscious mind, this is good news. If you aren't, then you're allowing your environment and circumstances to continuously openly plant seeds of failure in your subconscious mind. And that's bad news.

Consider the story of the chicken-eagle named Peter. Peter is an eagle and for some strange reason, he was hatched in a chicken farm under the care of a loving and accepting mother hen. He grew up in the midst of chickens and as such, was programmed to believe he was one even if it became pretty obvious he wasn't by the time he was an adolescent. One day, while playing in the farm with the other chickens, they saw an eagle flying above. Peter and the other chickens' beaks (they don't have jaws) fell to the floor in awe and admiration. What a majestic and powerful bird, they exclaimed. Peter's heart was stirred – he wanted to be like that eagle and soar! But, you guessed it right, his subconscious mind resulted in a collection of habits (paradigms) that were consistent with the belief that he's a chicken. And so, as much as he wanted to fly – and fly he can! – he couldn't. His chicken paradigm prevents him from realizing his potential.

Let's call the lion Simba. As he grew up in a farm, he acquired a paradigm of a domestic animal – tame and gentle. One day, Simba and the other farm animals took a break from grazing in the field by taking a drink on the riverbank. From out of nowhere on the other side, a lion appeared. He looked fierce and strong and roared a thunderous and powerful roar, which scared the living daylights out of the animals including

Simba! They all scampered back to the safety of the farm, shivering in fright.

After a few days, feeling it was safe, they went back to grazing in the fields. Once again, the lion appeared – this time from the bushes – and roared a mighty roar! Once again, they scampered back. This time, however, Simba felt rather weird: he was both drawn to the lion but at the same time afraid of it.

It happened again later on. But this time, Simba was so scared to run he wanted to scream. He did but only a pitiful sound came out, since his paradigm was that of a domesticated animal. As the other lion continuously roared at him, Simba panicked even more and screamed and screamed until he was able to roar! That's when he realized he wasn't a domesticated animal. He was a lion! From that point on, he left the farm and followed the other lion into the jungle and lived as he ought to in the first place: a mighty lion!

In both stories, the environments they grew up in planted and nurtured seeds of failure, i.e., acting contrary to their soaring and powerful natures. Never mind that they were built to soar to great heights or as kings of the jungle...their paradigms prevented them from fulfilling their destinies. Simba was fortunate because the other lion kind of forced him to change his paradigm and eventually become the powerful creature he was meant to be.

THE POWER OF CONSISTENCY

In as much as mango seeds planted in rich soil don't immediately grow up and bear fruit but require time and continuous exposure to sunlight and adequate water, so it is with paradigms. You'll need to continuously impart suggestions or thoughts of success to your subconscious mind, which will lead to bearing fruits of success paradigms.

His drunkard paradigm didn't develop overnight. It was developed through years of exposure to a drunkard father with whom he and his brother lived. He saw his father drunk and act the way he did every day as a child. That was what his subconscious mind was being fed every day. Drunkenness was the seed that was sown in his young but fertile soil of the mind, which was consistently nurtured through continued and repeated exposure.

Remember this: your conditioning, environment and eventually success or failure are highly influenced by what you always think about. Repetition is the strongest way of reinforcing a paradigm.

TERROR BARRIER TO LIFE CHANGES

If changing our lives through changing our paradigms is as simple as changing our subconscious thinking, why is it then that most people fail at it? The reason?

Fear.

"The cave you fear to enter holds the treasure you seek." – Joseph Campbell

Fear is the barrier, a terror barrier that keeps people from moving forward with changing their lives for the better. It may be one that's keeping you from doing the same too.

You may ask, "Why would I fear moving forward to a much better life?" The truth is, it's not the goal that you fear. It's the fear of failure, what other people will say about you and even fear of leaving your comfort zone.

The fear of failure is probably the most and common fear that's plaguing people right now. Some of my male friends failed to enjoy what could possibly be great relationships with women they were very much interested in because they fear being turned down or shunned away. Because of fear of failure, they didn't even try!

Many people wish for particular dream jobs or careers. However, the fear of being rejected or being unable to perform at the level required for such jobs or careers keeps them from taking advantage of any open opportunities - they were too afraid to even apply for their dream jobs or shift careers.

When it comes to changing paradigms, fear also keeps people from doing so. They're so afraid of the "consequences" of both success and failure that they don't try to work on their paradigms. Even if they have changed their paradigms, fear can make them go back to the old ones.

Another fear that keeps people from experiencing lasting changes and success is that of other people's opinions. This is most pronounced in people-pleasers. Their subconscious minds hold on to the value of what other people think of them and thus result in paradigms that do just that, including sticking to old but limiting and harmful paradigms. Consider alcoholics who developed the addiction to liquor by starting to drink in their teenage years in order to be considered "cool" and be part of the "in" crowd.

Lastly, the fear of discomfort can be a barrier towards changing for the better and succeeding in life. In today's society that values instant and self-gratification more than anything else, discomfort is something to avoid at all costs. Success, however, requires a price and often times at the beginning, that price is discomfort. As with fear of failure and other people's opinions, fear of discomfort keeps people from even trying to change, give up in the middle or go back to old paradigms after experiencing success.

Chapter 9 Achieving Quality and Natural Sustainability

The real starting point for my personal search for better ways to develop organizations was the poor quality I witnessed in the change programs I worked on. Naturally, then, I wanted to devote a chapter of this book to the quality of organizational change in relation to co-creation.

Later in this chapter I'll be introducing a simple guideline aimed at helping to ensure high-quality implementation. If you were to ask me how organizations can make the biggest difference in delivering quality changes, my answer would be that it's definitely about the quality of the implementation, not so much the quality of the idea.

In fact, I rarely come across ideas that simply seem stupid. They might not be perfect but, in most cases, they form a reasonable starting point for successfully developing change. Where I have seen a consistent shortfall is in the *implementation* of those ideas. This chapter focusses on how co-creation can help organizations raise the quality of their change programs.

Better Quality
Co-creation has a clear and simple advantage: simply by introducing this approach, an organization can improve the quality of what it offers, whether these are services or products. But it can also lead to better and more appropriate ways of working and smoother change programs. The more – and more diverse – the brainpower that goes into co-creation, the more the quality of the organization will improve.

To get the most out of the different perceptions of different people, it's useful to be as unbiased as possible. To judge nothing, either in a positive or negative sense. To respect and appreciate all views. To be as open as possible and to be inspired by others around you – all of them great thinkers and creators, just as you are.

As we'll see, this approach enables growth not just in terms of quality but also in when it comes to the sustainability of an organization.

More Brainpower, More Views

The principles are simple. Two people see and know more than one. A hundred more than fifty. Getting input from different people on what would be useful and appropriate solutions will improve the quality of these. And this inclusiveness is the default when an organization is based on co-creation.

These days, even in organizations that are managed top-down, people's input is requested on many occasions. But the results are often not as good as they could be – and that's because this input isn't obtained through co-creation.

By that, I mean that input is gathered in a pre-defined manner at a specific time, and is not unconditional. It is done in a conditional manner within the set structures of that organization, and the rules of the game are defined from the top. People can share their views – but only as long as they comply with management's expectations.

By contrast, co-creation aims to be a process of unconditional sharing of ideas and inspiration, and one in which there are few boundaries. The outcome is more fruitful, as it can draw on "out of the box" thinking that has not been pre-defined by the top-down approach.

What's more, people working in a co-creative organization are more open to sharing their ideas, as they understand this to be common practice. Their ideas are treated with respect and always matter –not just when they match the conditions set at the top.

Diverse Brainpower

Including more people will, by itself, lead to more diversity in co-creation. And it's not just through an increased number of views but also through this automatic gain in *diversity* of views that organizations will improve quality.

Diversity management is an area that's getting quite a bit of attention these days. Organizations are actively pursuing greater diversity through the inclusion of "different" people. The driver behind this type of approach is a social equality perspective – which is fine, of course.

But there's another way of looking at diversity: as an important basic ingredient for successful creations. And diversity is not something that necessarily needs to be actively pursued. Because diversity is all around us! Having many people working in an organization provides diversity by default – and very likely this will be what's required by the organization.

When people are allowed to be their authentic selves, the organization will have the diversity it needs. Authenticity in this sense is about being who you are and being in touch with your life purpose. This includes being free from the expectations created through your job description or the fact that you're active in a specific role.

Opposing Opinions

Diversity and opposing opinions go hand in hand. Opposing opinions have a special function. They provide contrast, are a source of clarity and in the end they play an important part in growth.

For example, an opinion that contrasts with your own can show you how your product might need to be further developed, enabling you to gain clarity on what has to be done. People and organizations develop and grow through this process. Embrace it.

Contrast is simply one of the mechanisms of the co-creation process. In fact, the more opposition there is, the faster the creative process can work. Opposition takes you out of your comfort zone and asks for your attention and a creative response. A nagging contrast often prompts people to "jumpstart" to a solution.

When you fight opposing opinions you don't have the time, clarity and energy to focus on what you do want – the thing that can provide you with joy and pleasure. That's when you need to remember that if you know what you *don't* want, this means you also know what you *do* want! Otherwise, you wouldn't be feeling this opposition so keenly. The trick is to use this opposition as an indication of what you really want.

Increase First Time Right
Co-creation allows you to arrive at 'first time right' solutions more often, as it tends to develop simple, successful solutions that are supported by all. By contrast, organizations that develop top-down solutions often suffer from what I call the 'cauliflower' syndrome.

Want improved quality? Learn to be a lazy leader!

I was hired by a customer to take on the role of Program Manager, responsible for implementing a business change within a specific area of their organization. In this role, I became aware of the fact that my needs and insecurities were a risk for the program's quality.

Basically, we had been successful in the initiation of the program and had all the right resources in place for a successful implementation, all the right people acting to their roles and responsibilities. The pro-gram went well and I was challenged to back off, to give space to these people and their qualities.

The challenging part for me was that there simply wasn't a whole lot left for me to do other than consult with the team and reassure them when they asked for help.

Being an external consultant, naturally I felt that I had to continue showing my added value. But in this case, when I did so it resulted in a loss of quality rather than an increase. I had to learn to bite my tongue, to trust others and be at peace with the fact that things would work out well without me.

But this also meant embracing the fact that my quality, in this case, was mainly my presence, my being rather than my skills. I had to learn to be a lazy leader.

This hands-on experience has made it much easier for me to recognize cases where leaders are hindering quality rather than adding to it – all with the best of intentions, of course!

An organization implements a solution thought up by a selected group of people. It has flaws and has only limited support from the bigger group who have to actually put it into practice. And the result is that it does not achieve what was originally intended. It needs to be adjusted – but once again this happens through the principle of top-down decision making. So the fix to the problem once again turns out to be sub-optimal.

In this way, organizations keep growing complex solutions, rather like the bulbs of a cauliflower. As a result, complexities multiply within the organization and its people have to spend a lot of time, energy and money to resolve the negative effects of top-down decision making.

This situation can only come about in organizations where processes and ways of working are implemented and managed from the top down. Because the people that execute them lack the required ownership and sense of responsibility to keep these ways of working lean and mean, and in sync with reality.

They just do as they're told, and if it's broken – well, it's broken. "Someone" – not them – has to fix it. It's important to realize that it's not the managers or co-workers who are to blame for this situation. It's simply a property of all structures that are organized from the top down

It's true that it has become more common to include customers, suppliers and other stakeholders outside the organization in the co-creation process. But to date, this kind of inclusion is restricted to product development, marketing and sales initiatives. It hasn't yet fed through into organizational development.

Co-created Solutions Are Easy To Implement

Another no brainer with co-creation: it's essential to include the people who are involved in or responsible for implementing the idea. This avoids the resistance that will typically come from them not having been involved.

They spend their time working in the area in which the idea will be introduced, and they care about it. It's more than likely that they feel passionately about this area, and they've almost certainly spent lots of time thinking about how things in it could be improved. They're in a position to create simple solutions. You can tap into their creativity, which is focused on exactly the area you need to develop.

Co-creation doesn't just mean that you'll come up with better solutions. It will also make it easier to materialize them. Because the very same people who have thought of the solution will be the ones putting it into practice. It's their idea.

Any high-quality solution is the combination of a well thought idea and the proper execution of that idea. To put it into a simple formula: success = quality of idea + quality of execution.

Diversity and Sustainability

The sustainability of an organization is closely related to the way it uses the available diversity within it. As we've seen, diversity comes by default from the people within the organization being authentic to themselves and being in touch with their life purpose. People like this are in better contact with their talents and creative ideas, which in turn means that these are available for the benefit of the organization.

Within a co-creative organization, such authentic people thrive and can contribute their creativity. Openness and active inclusion of authentic people in co-creation ensure a diverse mix of ideas.

Be less problem- / solution-oriented

One time when working for a client, I was asked to share my view on a supposedly problematic situation within a particular department. The department was said to be underperforming and there were issues to do with its cooperation with other key departments.

This manager felt he had to fix this problem. His first reaction was to go hire an expert to solve the problem. How? By creating structure. This is actually the natural reaction of a lot of people when they lack control of a situation and also lack the clarity needed to understand it fully.

In my conversation with this manager it became clear to me that he was not looking behind the issues. He was looking outside for solutions rather than inside for root causes. He lacked a clear understanding of the fact that the current situation was the exact result of what he and his team had created. Solutions had to come from him and his team – so something in the behavior of the team had to change.

Looking at the symptoms, it was obvious that there was indeed a lack of structure and of the basic tools needed for the job. It was like a bakery without an oven! So the really relevant question was: how did you ever get into this situation as a team? To me, there could be only two possible answers. The first being that the whole team and their leader were incompetent. The second, which I chose to believe, was that there were factors preventing the obvious, natural improvement from taking place. I suggested that the team and their leader to do some soul searching, dig beneath the symptoms and identify what the reasons were for them not yet having fixed the problem for themselves.

It took some challenging team sessions to identify and clear these blockages, but once this had happened the team implemented and embraced the necessary improvements by themselves.

In doing so, they created the conditions for lasting success. I believe the exact opposite would have happened if they had hired an external expert.

This results in an organization that will make things work. And this is the key to successful transformation: people whose attitude is all about wanting to make it work. Because the road towards successful transformation can be bumpy. Creativity and flexibility are required to respond to and deal with unforeseen events – and it's through co-creation that the necessary can-do attitude is achieved.

Agility

In the end, this diversity and flexibility results in more agile organizations that are ready to deal with whatever comes up more quickly and precisely. This kind of organization can also adapt faster, and in the end will be better able to create its own future through pro-active development.

Agility results in sustainability. As we don't always know what we'll come up against along the way, a diverse group of people that participate in both co-creation and co-materialization will deliver the best solutions to deal with the unknown. A mixed set of talents and views ensures this.

Sustainability in The Bigger Picture

Co-creation and diversity are excellent ways of creating a more sustainable organization. But this kind of sustainability will spread out to influence the wider environment of that organization as well.

When you're authentic, you're close to who you are. As a result you feel more connected to your environment. You are aware that you operate in a larger context which you influence and by which you are influenced – and that taking proper care of yourself has to include taking proper care of your environment.

Being authentic calls for self-love and self-respect. It's only from this perspective that it's possible to love and respect everything around you. Living and working sustainably is only natural from this position. It's simply painful to mistreat your environment, as you feel it to be part of you.

Organizational change is a subject that radiates an aura of negativity. It's seen as being difficult, as involving thorny issues of motivation, communication and so on. But these associations are just symptoms of deeper, underlying root causes – and when organizational change is approached in a different way they are seen for what they often are: just myths.

Chapter 10 Self-Worth

The dictionary describes self-worth as a sense of self or value as an individual. In this chapter, I will address the importance of real autonomy, how to construct that sort of autonomy, and why so many of us lack a sense of dignity.

Studies now indicate that based on external variables, the self-worth of your person is detrimental to your mind. One research at the University of Michigan discovered that students who base their autonomous value on external sources (including academic performance, appearance, and acceptance from others). They were also more alcohol, drug use, and eating disorders, as well as more symptoms of these conditions.

The same research discovered those who relied on their own inner voice felt not only better but also greater and less prone to drugs and alcohol and eating conditions.

Although true achievements are essential in recognizing you as building your feeling of self, the distinctive characteristics that create you should also take account of your self-worth. As an expert in consciousness, Dr. Donna Rockwell notes that we are all unique and intrinsic in each of us. "We shouldn't be evaluating ourselves, we should just be ourselves," says Dr. Firestone.

Self-Critique

The first step is to avoid comparing yourself and assessing each other; that is, you must challenge your critical internal voice. The critical inner voice is like a nasty trainer in our heads who always tosses us towards us or others with destructive ideas. This internalized dialogue of critical ideas undermines our feeling of being self-worth, even leading to self-destructive or unfitting behavior.

We all have a "cryptic internal voice" acting in our heads as a cruel coach who informs us that we are worthless or unworthy of happiness. Painful experiences influence the coach in our childhood, critical attitudes and emotions of our parents at an early age. Although these attitudes can be harmful, they have become an integral part of us over time. As adults, you might not see you as an enemy, but rather accept your own destructive viewpoint.

However, we can challenge the inner critic and not take his adverse position on ourselves and start to see ourselves for who we really are. We can distinguish our own emotions, ideas, wishes, and values and start to comprehend and appreciate them.

To kick off your journey to more profound self-love, start with these three steps:

Recognize your pain

In responding to pain, be kind and caring.

Remind yourself that imperfection is something we all share and is a component of the human experience.

Odds are you have come across "self "phrases — self-acceptance, self-esteem, and self-pity, etc. There are a lot of words to describe the way we feel, how we look at ourselves, and how we treat ourselves. If they all begin to mix for you, it's understandable, but they really are distinct ideas with distinctive purposes, results and meanings.

Although self-worth is often mistaken for self-esteem, self-worth is purely internal. Self-awareness can definitely contribute to self-worth. Knowing yourself and being self-reliant is something that can't be swayed by external factors. The same can't be said for self-esteem, which is more about the way we internalize how others see us.

To sum up, all that we think, feel, and trust in ourselves is self-esteem: I know that I am valuable likable and incomprehensible. Self-worth is realizing 'I am higher than all these things.'

The distinctions between self-worth and self-confidence are subtle as well.

Self-confidence isn't a general assessment of yourself, but rather a sense of trust and ability in various fields. For instance, in sports, there are topics you can talk, but you may have low confidence.

Similarly, there are subtle but important variations in one's self-worth There is no need for a strong sense of self-confidence in all fields of your lives; obviously, there are some things in which you will simply not be very nice and some other regions where you will be excellent. What is important is to have confidence and a high sense of authenticity in the activities in your life that matter to you.

The Psychology of the Self

When it comes to psychology, the perception of self-worth might be a less common subject compared to self-confidence and self-esteem.

Self-worth is at the heart of our own being — our ideas, sentiments, and conduct are closely connected with the way we regard our worth and value as human beings.

Based on the theory of self-worth, self-worth is mainly defined by self-assessment and the results in one or different operations which we consider to be important.

However, other standards are frequently used to evaluate their self-worth. Five of the most important variables for individuals to assess and compare themselves with the value of others are as follows:

How your body looks—whether measured by the figure on the scale, the kind of attention received by others. The net value this can generate, whether financial assets or material possessions. Your social network friends and the value of others based on their status and what is critical. Your

Your career—For instance, a stockbroker is often regarded as more prestigious than a janitor or teacher.

You are the only one who decides why they should be respected. You are worthy and wonderful and deserving of all the things you strive for.

Self-Worth in Relationships

One of the most common problems with low self-esteem is that you base your own self-worth on a specific element of your life—and that element often is a connection with another person.

It is an easily understandable tendency to allow someone else's affection to help you feel better about you. However, another person's love neither defines you nor defines your worth as an individual. You are worthy of love and respect, regardless of whether you are casually dating, single, or establishing a strong bond with another person, or just celebrated your 20th wedding anniversary with your spouse.

This is true about individuals with any relationship status but can be particularly crucial in long-term relationships.

You can better love someone else as a result of learning to love yourself. People who respect themselves tend to have relationships that are more satisfactory, more passionate and stronger than those who don't, exactly because they understand that first, they have to discover value, appreciation, and happiness within themselves.

Self-respect is the most vital aspect of one's life. Life is too short to expend energy on abusive or toxic relationships. For yours to flourish, you need to concentrate on loving yourself first.

Chapter 11 Meditation

I consider the way toward dealing with your brain during reflection of the 3Rs: Recognize, Release, and Return. You perceive when you have meandered from your place of center, discharge focusing on that "interruption," and come back to your picked object of consideration. It's that straightforward.

In any case, similar to any educated ability, it very well may challenge from the start. You may discover your mind meanders more often than not. You may end up got up to speed in negative considerations and sentiments. You may end up disturbed, self-basic, exhausted, or thinking about whether you're doing it right-or in case you're doing anything by any means!

That is OK. Perceiving the majority of this is a piece of reflection. Reflection expands mindfulness. You do this by carefully concentrating, perceiving and tolerating what your brain does, discharging interruptions, and coming back to your picked center over and over and once more.

As you rehash this procedure, you build up a feeling of simplicity by dealing with your musings and sentiments and an opportunity to pick what you center around and what you discharge. By rehearsing care during contemplation, you develop your capacity to identify with a wide range of minutes in your existence without breaking a sweat.

Further Benefits of Practice

As you ponder for a while (state 10-20 minutes) reliably, your mind calms down, your feelings quiet, and your body unwinds. You de-pressurize, let go of over-thinking, and discharge developed pressure. As you discharge pressure, vitality is opened up that your body and mind use to recuperate, fix, coordinate, and mend.

You begin to feel like yourself once more. You understand that "what your identity is" is significantly more than "the prattle" in your brain or the feelings that can "take you over." You are a more profound seeing nearness who "has" musings, sentiments, and encounters, however, isn't characterized by them. This can be a life changing revelation!

These advantages don't occur on the grounds that you are attempting to clear your psyche, they occur because of rehearsing the 3Rs. As you practice reliably, you build up the abilities of perceiving where your psyche is engaged, discharging what isn't serving you or others, and coming back to what is important most.

These are priceless abilities that serve you in anything you need to do, survive, or achieve. I would venture to such an extreme as to state they are crucial aptitudes you have to carry on with your life well. Why, at that point, would you say you weren't encouraged these fundamental abilities in school when you were youthful? Notwithstanding the reasons, at any age, you can learn them with a couple of basic guidelines, understanding how they work and steady practice.

Actually, I like to rehearse before anything else. For quite a bit of my life, I woke up inclination on edge about what I needed to do in the day ahead. However, presently, regardless of how I feel when I wake up, I feel loose and focused after my morning practice. I have a quiet reference point I can come back to when I get aggravated or worried, made up for lost time in antagonism, or feel overpowered by what's going on in my general surroundings.

Why Mindfulness and Meditation: Importance

Today there are interminable requests on our time, vitality and consideration and they call us all day, every day making us feel as though we generally should accomplish something profitable. We feel constrained to react in a split second via web-based networking media and accumulate a constant flow of tempting bits of data to keep us educated and interested. Indeed, even amusement turns into an "absolute necessity do" as we feel constrained to marathon watch to get "made up for lost time" with however much pleasure as could be expected in our "spare time."

However Continually Being "in A Hurry" Isn't Sound.

Our bodies and minds are not made to keep running in consistent overdrive. We are intended to participate in movement, at that point to rest and recuperate from what we've done. In our vacation, our body fixes itself, coordinates all that we've encountered, and recuperates cell harm we've continued.

Once we don't respect this equalization, our frameworks go haywire. We get depleted, hold expanding levels of pressure in our bodies, and become industriously restless or discouraged. In this "overcooked" state, we welcome the host of incessant ailments like malignant growth, coronary illness, and auto-invulnerable issue that are scourge.

Contemplation is an organized break from this action, so you can concentrate internally, rest, and recoup. From the start, it might want to do "nothing," be that as it may, as we've seen, the procedure is a delicate, yet dynamic, preparing of your brain. It enables you to step over from the frenzied pace of life, deliberately loosen up, and see what's happening inside.

Reflection and care uncover your internal operations. They reveal the intuitive predispositions that lead to contentions, misguided thinking, and terrible choices. They sparkle a light on propensities that drive undesirable outcomes throughout your life. They help you all the more impartially see what you are doing, so you can intentionally pick solid propensities and let go of unfortunate ones.

Possibly in particular for us in this hyper-driven buyer culture, they urge us to back off, take a full breath, and focus on the connections, blessings, and openings we as of now have, as opposed to continually attempting to be, have, and accomplish more.

Meditation and Mindfulness Dangerous: The End Approach

Are reflection and care risky? Indeed. They take steps to make you progressively cognizant and deliberate. They are risky to your negative musings, emotions, practices, and convictions. They discharge the smothering grasp of dread, predisposition, and bias. They sparkle a light on what requirements to change.

By rehearsing care in contemplation, you figure out how to assess all sides of any circumstance all the more unbiasedly, so you can settle on better choices. You perceive what never again serves you and others, so you can move your time, vitality, and regard for what does. What's more, you become progressively present, centered, and completely occupied with your encounters, so you carry on with a more extravagant, increasingly deliberate life.

Your Mind Is Your Greatest Power

Thus, we should attempt to clarify why your brain is your most prominent power. Everything in our universe, just as such seems stable in our physical world, is comprised of vibrations of vitality. Indeed, even our considerations are made by these vibrating waves, and are the most unique and liquid substance in the whole universe.

Is it accurate to say that you are directing your heart to thump at the present time? Assuming no, what does? How can it impact you?

To start with, your contemplations are autonomous of the physical universe, but then it communicates with it. Is astounding that any idea that is rehashed again and again in your cognizant personality will at that point make an engraving into your subliminal.

Furthermore, when this imprint makes it into your oblivious personality, it is then utilized as a tuning device and starts vibrating and draws into you the individuals, the conditions, and the occasions that match the pictures that you have inside. You have a genuine capacity to impact and direct the things that transpire.

Influence: The Power To subdue

In this way, let me make a point before you consider me in dismay. It is hard for you to think about that you can accomplish certain things or are adequate or effective or rich. However, you accept the inverse to be valid. Hence, for what reason would it be unimaginable for your brain to trust one way yet not the other?

A lovely aspect regarding the subliminal and its capacity is that it can't differentiate between what is genuine and what you envision. So it implies that you can program and engraving into it anything you need.

Thus, tests have been done about this where competitors fundamentally envision rehearsing for a month and after that do just as the individuals who did to be sure practice. It brought about their mind accepting that they were great which improved their presentation. Hence, envisioning an activity or a condition of being in your brain, again and again, makes a significant engraving on your subliminal.

The Powerful Source Within

The Soviet Union utilized it on their competitors, I know, I was one of them. Be that as it may, what is significantly more prominent is that it goes past game and can be utilized for accounts, connections, vocation, and self-mending. There are no parts of your life unthinkable when you work with mind control techniques. It tends to be representation, pondering, certifications, fascination or making new convictions. You have a feeling that you assume responsibility for your life.

Your considerations are the most staggeringly amazing wellspring of sustenance and wealth. In any case, no one shows us how to think. We figure out how to be certain or do as well as can be expected. All things considered, I am heartbroken, yet that is tragic. Positive reasoning is principal while mind power is an incredible asset available to you.

Furthermore, the laws and techniques can be promptly comprehended by anybody. It is a genuine arousing once you understand that your musings impact your world. Once you do have confidence at the top of the priority list control, you are in front of a huge number of different people, since despite everything it is basically an ongoing hypothesis. Just a little level of the world puts stock in it, and half of those don't rehearse it every day or in the correct manner.

Mind Power: Definition

Mind power isn't simply being sure; it is utilizing approaches to engrave convictions and pictures, not just on a cognizant level all things considered with positive intuition however on an oblivious level. When you envision and live the stuff you need, over and over, you are pulling in those things to you.

Furthermore, there is no more prominent defining moment in your life than to find that you have an individual power and that you are the ace of your predetermination. And everything necessary is possibly fifteen minutes per day to change your life once you are prepared to rehearse day by day.

In any case, recall that it can work similarly against you. The explanation being is that your considerations can likewise keep you in neediness, in ailment or not prevail at your objectives. Indeed, it is probably the best disaster of today. It is the reason the vast majority are not excelling. Their mind control intuitively pulls in an inappropriate things in their lives. In truth, your contemplations are what is making your world.

Mind Power and Creativity

Imaginative individuals frequently produced developments through thoughts appearing unexpectedly, however consistently when they took a break. These things don't occur when you are excessively occupied or buckling down. You should give yourself great quality time and respect yourself. So you have to take opportunity days where you don't work by any stretch of the imagination.

What's more, when you let go of everything, you give a period your inventiveness and instinct to connect with the wealth of contemplations and mind influence you have at your mien.

For what reason do I generally get my best thoughts in the shower?

In this way, even a little league away can have any kind of effect. Today, I am a major devotee to simply getting some much needed rest sometimes to reflect, survey and assess things. In the event that you pull in the things that are at a similar recurrence you are the point at which you are pushed or exhausted, it won't benefit you in any way.

Accomplish Something You Love

You are a splendid human machine with mind control! What I have acknowledged is that every single fruitful individual I know made their fortune and met accomplishment in a zone that they cherished. Think for a second! Has anybody at any point made a lot of cash by accomplishing something that they abhor?

I without a doubt don't! Steve Jobs got into PCs since he adored it and needed to have any kind of effect, not on the grounds that he needed to be rich. That is one of the privileged insights of achievement also. So discover something that you want to do. In addition to the fact that you will be progressively fruitful at it you will have a ton of fun doing it.

Along these lines, you win the two different ways. However, one of the adages of mind power is that you should comprehend what you need before you can get it. Furthermore, you need to ensure that your objectives are joined to a strategic, or reason, or it won't last.

Chapter 12 Be Prepared Without Obsessing

People worry expecting something bad to happen. Worrying becomes a security blanket that deals with the threat that the future is likely to bring. It is not a bad thing, but when your anxiety grows as a result of your desire to control future events; you suffer the consequences of your obsession.

Worrying in this light becomes very tiring because no matter how strong you are, you cannot control the future. You can plan for various eventualities but at the end of it all, your obsession is only going to exhaust you.

Planning vs. Worrying

Are you planning or worrying? It is always good to be pre-plan and prepare because it helps you deal with the outcome. The negative aspect of planning is that when you become too obsessed with controlling the outcome, you get completely overwhelmed by your anxiety.

It is important to plan because it helps keep things in order, but you should be aware of the boundaries so that you are sure that your planning is still proper:

Planning	Worrying
Listing ways to positively achieve certain outcome	Listing how ill-prepared you are for a future catastrophe
Making step-by-step action plan	Trying to conquer all aspects of the problem simultaneously in an effort to overcome it
Recognizing things that you can and cannot control	You are obsessing over things you cannot control, in an effort to control them
Making plans towards fulfillment of things that you can control	You are getting frustrated and fearful about your lack of control
You are prepared to seek assistance from others, if necessary	You are certain about not needing assistance of others and if ever, you will delay asking for help till the last minute

Looking at the table above, are you a worrier or a planner? Are you crossing the boundary of obsessing over threats and danger, to the point that you are completely overwhelmed by your emotions?

Writing Your Worry Diary

A good way to assess if you are obsessing is to keep track of your behavior with the help of a 'worry diary'. You see, worrying is not a bad thing. But when you are already obsessing, it can be very disruptive and destructive.

A 'worry diary' is like any journal. It is meant to keep a record for the purpose of tracking. How do you maintain this 'worry diary'?

Step 1: Write down all your worries. Do not be afraid to elaborate what you feel. Write down all your worries in an effort to declare them and by doing so, you will release it and unburden yourself.

Step 2: Clarify your thoughts. After declaring your worries, it is time for you to understand the depth of your problems so you can determine which ones are worth your attention. Are your fears and worries legitimate? What is the likelihood of these things to happen?

Step 3: Challenge your thoughts. After examining every single worry you have, face them head-on by challenging them. The problem with most people is that they let their worries destabilize them and thereby get stuck in a helpless position. Scrutinize your worries to understand them thoroughly and then you can effectively deal with them. Consider all possible solutions to your dilemma and imagine the worst case scenario.

Step 4: Reframe your worries. At this point, you should have a better understanding of your worries and anxieties, so that you can reframe them in a more realistic sense. Your worries do not have to be the endpoint of all things. There is a way that you can strategically conquer all your worries so that they do not win over you. By reframing your worries, you give them a different outlook, so that they no longer feel so threatening.

Being prepared is always an asset. It allows you to be more systematic, but at the same time, it encourages obsession. When your planning takes this course, it is no longer healthy. It is therefore important, that you keep yourself in complete touch with your emotions so that you can handle them efficiently and effectively.

Live Today

The threat of dreadful things to come will always bring enough reasons to worry. Future events that threaten to come in a catastrophic manner have the influence to overcome us. The very definition of worrying is, "causing anxiety about actual or potential problems". It may not have happened yet, but it has already disarmed you. Is that healthy?

Some people will argue that worrying allows them a level of preparedness.

The threat of future events may be real but you should not allow yourself to be entrapped by them. The consequence of this is neglect of the present.

Threats of The Past

The future can be ominous but the past brings poison. Some people are not necessarily consumed by the unknown future, but they are unable to let go of their past. They become a prisoner of their past pains, defeats and suffering and consequently become reluctant to move forward.

Are you afraid of the shadows that hide in your past? Sometimes the past represents mistakes and errors that brought destruction—it causes someone to be wary and defensive. No one wants to repeat their mistakes. Worrying about the past is extremely natural because past events have a way of adversely affecting the present and future events. But dwelling on the past is not going to change the outcome of things that have already happened, so you should focus on the present because at the moment that is what matters most.

Living in The Present

Sure there are potential dangers looming over you. Of course, anything can go wrong. Being oblivious to the danger of the future is irresponsible and carelessness but abandoning the present is more ridiculous.

You have to make a decision to live in the present because:

1. It will teach you to be more forgiving. It teaches you to be more grateful for what you are today, and gently releases any regrets or grudges that you may carry from the past. Everyone has scars to show, but not everyone is able to forget the intensity of pain it represents.
2. It will give you a sense of fulfillment. Life can throw anything in your direction. If you do not acknowledge it, you will lose the opportunity. There is so much life has to offer but sadly, people miss most of it because they don't pay attention. If you keep your eyes open to the present—you will experience life in its best form, and always feel complete, happy, cheerful and fulfilled.
3. It will take care of your worries. Living in the present is like leading an active life that is focused on accomplishing day-to-day functions. You want to get things done and you focus on them, so your worries automatically get blocked, even without you knowing it.
4. It will make you feel free. People are too overcome with expectations, past happenings and worries. These things can weigh quite heavily and can greatly affect your life by confining you within the boundaries. By letting go of your past and living the present moment, you will feel much better. It will feel as though your world just got bigger and less demanding.
5. It will help avoid disappointments. When you are living within strict boundaries and are compelled to meet expectations, there is a greater chance for you to encounter failures and disappointments. Living in the present makes you feel free, and also happier. It is easier

to get upset when a list of unreasonable expectations is not met, so let go of all these boundaries.
6. It will open you up to better relationships. Positivity attracts people and living the moment opens your life to the world in a 'can-do' attitude that many people appreciate and admire.
7. It will make you happier. Worries can work as obstacles. When you allow them to inundate you, they can overcome you to the point of destroying you. Worry and anxiety are like poison and when you choose to live in utmost toxicity, your life will feel heavy. But when you choose to live in the moment, you will feel lighter and happier.
8. It will make you more accepting of the unpredictable. The future is extremely unpredictable. There is no way for you to know what's going to happen, and so you have the tendency to obsess on trying to control everything. When you learn to start living in the present, you become more accommodating and tolerant of events, irrespective of how unpredictable they are. Unpredictability is frightening but your fears don't have to overwhelm you.

The past and the future are important, but your present needs your full focus and attention. The problem with most people is that they are either trapped in their past or are threatened by their future. Both distant but the obsession of the past and future takes the focus away from the present which matters the most.

How To Live Today

By now you should have a better understanding of how important your present is, so you will need to focus. The past is instrumental in formatting your present and the future is the fulfillment of your past and present days. The future is the final destination and it is natural to obsess on the details, but you have to learn to prioritize.

You choose to live today because your present is more important than the growing threat of your worries and anxieties.

Step 1: Let Go. You have to let go of your past, however painful it is; and you have to surrender your future. You have to accept that there are certain things that you cannot change or control, so just let go. There is no point in obsessing about these things.

Step 2: Savor It. Life is too beautiful for you to simply take it for granted. Your present life is there for you to savor and enjoy so allow yourself to experience it. Why are you so worried about the past and the future, when what matters is the present moment? Experience every moment as it unfolds and this will allow you to perceive life in a different way.

Step 3: Practice Mindfulness. Mindfulness represents your ability to clear your mind of the negativity so that you can focus. To live the moment, you have to be fully aware of the happenings around you. This will allow you to elicit appropriate responses for various situations, and it is achieved through meditation. Mindfulness is easily transformative.

Step 4: Enjoy the Flow. You have to take things one-at-a-time. It is not easy to let go of the past and stop worrying about the future, but if you are sincere about your desire to control your anxiety, you have to learn to go with the flow. You have to learn to go with the flow so that you can focus on the moment and the take events as they fall into your lap.

Step 5: Be Accepting. There is a level of maturity displayed in one's ability to accept. Accept pains and hurts. Acknowledge things you cannot do and cannot control. Accept outcomes irrespective whether they are favorable or not. Acceptance shows a level of maturity as it signifies your ability to accept things as they are and move on.

Step 6: Experience and Engage. More than just going with the flow and taking life as it comes, you have to engage it. You have to take an active part in your life and not be a mere spectator. To gain a better appreciation of the moment, you have to engage. You have to choose to be in the front and center of the happenings so that you are in total control.

Step 7: Take Action. Do what needs to be done today. When you talk about living the moment, it involves taking action. It means that you have to take the step that actually keeps the ball rolling. You shouldn't waste any more time dwelling on the past that you cannot change; and you should not worry about controlling the future because no matter how much you worry, the only thing that matters is the present.

You live today because the truth is that time is gold and if you dwell too much in the past and future, you will not be able to catch the present. If you are not careful, time will slip away and you will just lose it. To be able to exist in the moment, you have to be in complete control and find perfect focus.

Conclusion

By practicing all the above affirmations daily, you will find that gradually your mind is being cleansed and your aura is becoming free of all impurities. I hope you become unbiased, strong, pure, positive and free from all fears. By gaining knowledge on all topics mentioned you will learn how to tackle your mind to balance it between stress and happiness. Don't lodge subconscious mind with any negativity.

Practice all the exercises and good habits to maintain your physical and mental health. After reading this book you should have complete control on your thoughts and desire for filling it with all the positive assertions. Make your personality strong that no evil can contaminate you. Keep laughing every day and spread love and joy to all your loved ones. Be stable and calm so that you don't linger between the extremes. Fill your heart with joy and not with grief of sorrow and misery. Always be close to God, he is the controller of our life. Do good deeds because sooner or later the day will come when we have to answer him about our actions.

I hope that my readers enjoyed this book. I wish you always remember all the tips I suggested for being happy and positive throughout your life. Recall all the positive affirmations regularly and practice all the exercises every day to maintain good health.

Third Eye Chakra

A Guide for Beginners to Unlock The Secrets of Chakras Balance, Meditation and Third Eye Awakening Including Some Reiki Self Healing Techniques to Increase Energy and Cure Your Body

[Joseph Brain]

Introduction

The third eye chakra is called the Ajna Chakra in Sanskrit and is in charge of our intuition. The third eye concept itself is all about seeing whether that means physically seeing or seeing something within ourselves. The third eye chakra acts as our inner eye and helps us interpret the workings of the world so that we may be better equipped to make decisions and move through this life. All of this intuition will lead you to have a powerful inner guidance system that stems from the energies and experiences of the third eye chakra. Since the third eye chakra is one of the most powerful chakras in our bodies, it is associated with the energies of the Sun itself.

The third eye chakra also helps us recognize the Divine in the most human way possible. We are unable to attain the Divine head while we are still moving through life on this Earth, but the third eye helps us at least interpret the Divine while we are here. In Hinduism, the primary goal of life is to escape the cycle of reincarnation, or rebirth, and unite your soul with the Divine God Head. For that reason, the chakras help us make the most of our lives on this Earth so that we may be as free of sin as possible. Once you have attained full control over all your desires, actions, and lifestyle, you may be able to join as one with the Divine. Thus, you will escape the cycle of rebirth and grief that lives on through the rest of the beings and souls on Earth. The third eye is the closest connection we have to God - thus, we must fully trust the intuition and guidance this chakra provides us with.

In addition to having a much more spiritual purpose, the third eye chakra is also invested in helping you heighten your capacity for creativity, wisdom, and insight. The third eye oversees your external environment but is also able to look inward to judge and boost the energies of the chakras that lie below it. The third eye chakra helps add slight adjustments to the workings and purposes of each of the lower 5 chakras so that you may fully align with your purpose and soon be united with the Divine God Head. In turn, you will receive a great amount of peace and self-confidence. If you heal and rely on your third chakra with no doubts in your mind, you will be able to reap all the benefits of a soul that is moving towards moksha (freedom from the cycle of rebirth) and eternal happiness with the Divine. The third eye chakra will ultimately take you to your true purpose.

Third Eye Chakra Color and Function

The third eye chakra is located in the space between your eyebrows and is represented by the color indigo. Indigo, or royal blue, is the color we most closely associate with wisdom and deep inner knowledge. When we appeal to this color, we will find that a different part of ourselves is awakened. We come more spiritual, and the door to the Divine becomes unlocked for us to someday walkthrough. This is because indigo is the color that bridges the Earth with the Heavens, and thus bridges life and death.

Meditating on the indigo color of the third eye chakra will allow your senses and feelings to become more refined and clearer. The lower chakras all respond well to their specific colors, but parts of them also respond clearly to indigo. They will become more spiritually enlightened as they let the color of the third eye chakra wash over their energies and uplift their purposes. Indigo also acts as a lightbulb in your brain - helping you come up with powerful ideas to change the world and achieve your dreams. You will be able to unlock more and more pieces of your true self as you let indigo flood into your body and specifically into your third eye chakra.

As you can probably imagine, the third eye chakra is also associated with certain parts of the physical body that benefit from positive third eye chakra energies. The eyes, ears, nose, brain, pineal gland, pituitary gland, and large parts of the nervous system all partially depend on the third eye chakra for their functioning. So, if we are unable to achieve and maintain a full balance of the third eye chakra, it is likely that physical symptoms relating to these body parts may arise and disrupt your life. These symptoms will be signaling you that something is wrong with your chakra and that you need to take some time to balance your third eye. It is likely that these symptoms will fully disappear once you are able to promote healthy energy flow through the third eye chakra again.

Nature of Balanced Third Eye Chakra

The third eye chakra is first and foremost responsible for the broad spirituality you have within you. Since your sense of self-worth is so deeply tied to this energy wheel, you will feel extremely confident in your life path and purpose as your third eye chakra becomes more and more balanced. One of the biggest changes you will notice right away is your emotional stability. As challenges and hardships keep coming your way throughout your life, your third eye chakra will act as your support system and will empower you to see the bigger picture. As you are able to attribute life's hard moments to a bigger plan for your life, you will be able to move through those disruptions with more gracefulness and ease. Additionally, you will see a purpose in all of the hard times in your life, which will allow you to carry on without feeling overwhelmingly discouraged. Life will always, always have something difficult in store for you. If your third eye is balanced, you will feel secure in knowing that these challenges are here to teach you something or lead you on the path to something extremely good and necessary in your life.

Another major benefit of having a well-healed and functional third eye chakra is the overall balance it will introduce into your life. Most people can be characterized by the way they follow their emotions over logic and vice versa. If you have a completely aligned third eye chakra, you will have the strength and good sense to take information from both your emotional and logical minds and apply the knowledge to the particular situation at hand. In time, you will be able to hear both sides in your mind without being predisposed to choosing one over the other. This balance and careful reasoning will allow you to become more well-rounded in the ways you make decisions and the way you function as part of a two-person relationship.

In congruence with the way your sacral chakra helps you develop a better sense of self, your third eye chakra will help you further develop a strong sense of intuition that will nicely compliment the person you are becoming. Your intuition and gut feelings will be much more accurate, and so you will gain faith in your ability to perceive and navigate the world around you. As your intuition continues to develop, you will feel a more spiritual connection to your deeper purpose in life. Your gut will lead you to where you need to go, and you will confident knowing that your third eye chakra is taking you to exactly the right path and presenting you with exactly the right opportunities and circumstances. For that reason, you will no longer feel like your life is stagnant. You will be able to move forward with power and take the world by storm just as you are meant to. As you begin to meet your goals, you will feel an ever-deeper connection to your passions and overall purpose. This will form into a positive feedback loop that just continues to produce more and more of the positive result for you as your third chakra becomes more and more balanced and healthy.

I encourage you to fully trust the voices and energies in your mind and soul. Once everything is balanced from the crown of your head down to your root, you will be in full control of yourself. At this point, and especially with the balancing of your third eye chakra, you will notice a profound difference in how you feel about yourself and your life. You will be more motivated to live, love, and change the positive world you were born into.

Blocked Third Eye Chakra Symptoms & Self-Examination

If this is the case, it will be harder and harder to get back up on your feet the longer this energy blockage goes on. An overactive third eye chakra will generally result in a wild imagination that can lead to extreme dreams or nightmares. This is the result of the lack of grounding in reality that your third eye chakra is experiencing. On the other hand, an underactive third eye chakra might lead to you have a very limited way of thinking because you have poor intuition. You may experience learning or memory problems and even have difficulties with their imagination.

It is also very common for chakra imbalances to manifest into physical symptoms that can further disrupt your life. The physical symptoms of a third eye chakra blockage generally arise if the energies in your body have been blocked for a very long time. Thus, it is important to make sure that you take the physical symptoms of a third eye chakra imbalance just as seriously as you would take the physical symptoms from any other medical condition. This way, you will be able to help mind and body return to their most optimal and ideas states of functioning. If your third eye chakra is out of balance in one way or another, it is likely that you will feel some or even all of the following disruptions in your life:

Mental/Emotional Symptoms:

- Lack of faith
    - This symptom generally relates to your purpose and lacking faith in your plan. For example, if you are having a challenging time figuring out why you should keep pushing through hardships, or if

you have trouble seeing the good in your future plans, it is likely that you have a third eye chakra blockage

- PARANOIA

  - Frustration with your path
  - Feeling pointless
    - This goes along with lacking faith in your general purpose. If your third eye chakra is blocked or somehow malfunctioning, it will be extremely difficult for you to see through the muddled mess in your brain and have confidence in your spiritual plan. This symptom can look like many scenarios including feeling worthless or not seeing the point in relationships, your job, and in your life in general
  - Having trouble making decisions
  - Feeling like your life or work is insignificant
  - Feeling like there is no meaning to your life

Physical Symptoms:

  - Sinus pain

- MIGRAINES

- HEADACHES

  - Tension in your forehead and brow area
  - Discomfort in or around your eyes
  - Back pain
  - Leg pain or tingling

If your passion or vocation is criticized or somehow compromised, you will most likely feel the effects of a damaged third eye chakra. Since this chakra is primarily focused on our purpose in life and our spiritual plan, anything that threatens that security can trigger the third eye energies to go out of balance. The third eye is one of the most sensitive chakras in our system, and so any changes that cause you to rethink your life in any way can have disastrous effects on the emotions and physical symptoms the chakra controls. For that reason, we recommend having a consistent routine that promotes third eye chakra health so that it never has a need to go out of balance. When the chakra does become blocked, it is telling you that something is wrong and that you need to live something different than the way you are living it now. So, if you are able to fall in tune with your third eye chakra, anticipate the triggers coming your way, and continuously protect your energies, you will have a much more stable third eye. As a result, your faith and feelings of purpose will remain more or less stable throughout your life.

How To Awaken and Align The Third Eye Chakra

1. *Self-Affirmations:* Ancient and even modern studies have shown that our energy responds positively to mantras that we either repeat to ourselves or write down in visible places throughout the day. The self-affirmations have strong power, so it is important to keep in mind that these statements should contain no negativity and be fully reassuring. We want to combat the destructive and distorted emotions and thoughts in our minds with constructive and encouraging statements so our third eye chakra can recognize its full potential again and help boost our spiritual energy. These statements are simple reminders that tell us our surroundings are secure and help stabilize

damaged or misaligned chakras. Try using some of the following self-affirmations throughout your day if you have been feeling the effects of a blocked third eye chakra. Feel free to go beyond these examples and customize the statements to you and your current situation! Just remember that if you do choose to create your own self-affirmations, stick to the themes of self-purpose, spirituality, and instincts. This will help your statements specifically awaken your third eye chakra. Eventually, your third eye chakra will recognize the statements you use on a daily basis and will reflect the energy you are putting into your body and mind.

a) "My third eye is open, and I am able to see my purpose."
b) "I know my intuitions will lead me to my purpose."
c) "I believe that I am already on my true path."
d) "I have full trust in the guidance that my third eye gives me."
e) "I am confident in my ability to make the right decisions, and I can make them with ease."
f) "I live in accordance with my life's purpose every day."
g) "The possibilities that are open to me are endless."
h) "My intuition and spiritual energy are telling me what is right for me."

2. *Visualization:* All of our chakras respond well to visualizing the color of the chakra in the specific region of our body. For this chakra, it is also helpful to meditate on the different aspects of your life you hope to build up in the future. This can relate to you envisioning the perfect job, relationships, or any other goals you have for your life. Envisioning things

like this will help as you try to make them a reality in your life.
3. *Connect to Nature:* In order to help the nature and environment around you connect with your spiritual third eye chakra, try exploring the air you breathe, the mountains around you, the winter season, and any seemingly magical experiences like rainbows in the sky. Try also to be out in nature to experience the beginnings and ends of the life cycles for some of the plants and beings on Earth. This will help re-energize the throat chakra to drive you to your final and true purpose.
4. *Aromatherapy:* aromatherapy generally involves diffusing aromatic oils throughout your space or rubbing them directly onto specific pressure points on your skin. If you are experiencing symptoms of an underactive third eye chakra, try waking it up and stimulating its energy by inhaling or diffusing rosemary essential oil. If you feel like you may have a more overactive third eye chakra that needs to be calmed and restored to its optimal state, try using a milder oil like German chamomile oil. Frankincense and sandalwood oils have well-balanced aromas and will help maintain your smoothly functioning root chakra once you have already opened and cleared the energy wheel. Other aromas and essential oils that can be particularly beneficial for aligning your root chakra include angelic root, cypress, and marjoram oils. Since the third eye chakra supports your mental awareness and visionary capabilities, it can be beneficial to put a small amount of oil on your forehead where this chakra resides in the body.
5. *Nutrition:* All foods that we normally consider healthy will definitely help promote the wellbeing of

your chakras. However, there are some specific foods that you can integrate into our diets a little more in case you have been feeling the specific effects of a blocked third eye chakra. Try eating these foods a little more frequently because they are likely to help awaken and energize your third eye chakra.

    a. Omega-3 Foods: these are fats are sometimes called "healthy fats" and are well-known enhancers of cognitive function. That enhancement will, in turn, help balance the energies and functions of your third eye chakra. Foods that are high in Onega-3 fats include sardines, salmon, chia seeds, and walnuts.

    b. Dark Chocolate: this is the kind of chocolate you can eat with little to no guilt at all! Feel free to eat as much dark chocolate as you would like while you are actively trying to open or align your third eye chakra because dark chocolate is a great source of magnesium - a natural de-stressor. Dark chocolate will also help boost your mental clarity and concentration so that you can unlock the full powers of your third eye chakra. Lastly, dark chocolate also aids in your body's release of serotonin molecules that will help keep you more positive.

    c. Purple Foods: since the third eye chakra is connected with purple or indigo, eating foods of that color will help awaken your energy wheel and lead to its balance. Examples of purple foods you can try including eggplants, red grapes, blueberries, purple cabbage, and blackberries.

6. *Crystal Healing:* holding, wearing, or even placing crystal stones of jewelry throughout your space can be extremely beneficial to you as you try to align your

chakras and generate positive spiritual energy. If you are eager to see results and help balance your third eye chakra quickly, try holding a third-eye specific stone in the palm of your hand and giving it several squeezes so that its energies flow into your open body. Each chakra responds well to different stones because each of them has different healing properties that they desire and possess. The following three stones are mostly purple in color and will help you open up the third eye energy wheel.

a. Amethyst: This stone is a deeply purple shade and has been used many times over as a representation of wisdom. Amethyst is also deeply connected to all forms of healing, including headaches that can arise from a damaged third eye chakra.

b. Purple Fluorite: This purple stone has powers that can help increase your mental clarity and return the faculties of your mind back into your own self-control. The sharpened intuition you will reap by using this stone will help you, particularly when you are confused by many distractions and choices when trying to make an important decision.

c. Black Obsidian: This is a balancing stone that helps promote and equal partnership between emotions and reasons within your mind and soul. The third eye chakra responds well to this stone because it is full of balancing and soft power.

Secret Tips for Balancing The Third Eye Chakra

Most of the chakras in our bodies respond to similar techniques when it comes to healing. For example, crystal healing, meditation, and specific nutrition all benefit each of our chakras.

However, the third eye chakra is much more complex than the rest of the energy wheels in our system, and so there are some more tips and healing practices that can positively affect the third chakra. They are as follows:

1. *Keep an Open Mind:* The third eye is all about developing a strong intuition, and that can only truly happen if you are able to explore a variety of different viewpoints and perspectives. If you are closed-minded, you might be stifling the powers of your third eye chakra and not letting it reach its full potential. Try going out of your comfort zone to read articles or books or engage in other activities that will help expand your mindset and help broaden your perspective on the world.
2. *Meditate on OM:* "Om" is a syllable that is considered one of the most mystical and powerful mantras in Hinduism. This chant, when drawn out with a long breath and pronounced as "ommmmmmmm" until your breath runs out, will match the vibrational energies of the third eye chakra. This chant and meditation technique will certainly help awaken the spiritual energies of the third eye chakra.
3. *Observe Your Dreams:* Our dreams, and particularly our nightmares, are imaginative reflections of the deepest parts of our personalities. They can reflect our biggest fears, past traumas that we can't seem to move on from, or general needs and desires. If you are able to think about your dreams and nightmares in the morning once you wake up, it is likely that you will discover some pattern or message your subconscious is trying to make you aware of. Once you become more in tune with this subconscious, your third eye chakra will follow, and you will be able to harness its full powers.

4. *Pineal Gland Health:* The pineal gland is one of the parts of our body that can be affected by the energies of the third eye chakra. However, in this case, the third eye chakra can also reversely be affected by the health of the pineal gland. Historically, the pineal gland has mystical roots that go far beyond its general role in promoting better sleep and regulating our reproductive hormones. Try decalcifying your pineal gland by avoiding excessive amounts of calcium, pesticides, and other toxins like artificial sweeteners and sir fresheners. Once your pineal gland is completely healthy again, that will translate over into the health and proper functioning of your third eye chakra.
5. *Be in the Sun:* The element we most associate with the third eye is light and so as you can imagine, it is extremely beneficial for the third eye chakra if we are exposed to more natural light throughout our day. Light therapy will also help open up the pineal gland, which, as we just learned, is essential to the third eye chakra. Try to take a walk, play, or even just lay out in the sun for a few minutes more than you normally would in your day. This exposure will most definitely help you open your third eye chakra.

Chapter 1 Chakra Meditation

Maybe you consider reflection a demonstration of sitting leg over leg and murmuring to oneself. All things considered; this isn't all what contemplation is about. You will discover a wide range of types of contemplation that help you in unwinding and diminishing pressure. Chakra is a particular type of reflection which starts from Hindu convictions. Today, the specialty of chakra reflection has spread to each edge of the globe.

Chakra Meditation is a type of reflection that comprises a lot of unwinding procedures concentrated on bringing parity, unwinding and prosperity to the chakras. "Chakra" is an antiquated Sanskrit word that implies vortex or wheel that can be followed back to India.

Chakras are the human body's seven primary vitality focuses with every one relating to singular organs that administer our particular body parts in addition to different regions of the mind. They are situated alongside a hormonal organ along the human spinal segment.

Chakras can wind up blocked and if even one of the 7 Chakras ends up blocked, it sets us up for physical and passionate an issue which is something nobody needs.

How Do Chakra Meditation Techniques Work?

Our wonderful and puzzling universe circulates its awesome life-power vitality to the earth and to our organs and organs situated all through the body and circulatory system. This life-power vitality is key so as to acquiring ideal prosperity and wellbeing. It's accepted that since the chakras are interrelated, they intently influence each other, by attempting to accomplish the ideal degree of equalization.

Make Each Cell in Your Body Stir and Celebrate!

A large portion of us has vigorous squares and awkward nature just as vitality attacking propensities that keep us from getting to our full essentialness, which leads us to feel depleted, dispersed, dull... even sick.

The Benefits of Meditation

In the event that new to meditation, questions concerning a capacity to do it can surface, bringing up issues like "How would I consider nothing?" or considerations like "I can't do that." It can appear to be odd to attempt to discharge ourselves from the pending negative issues in life by a what may appear to be a straightforward demonstration of sitting idle, particularly when compelling passionate battles can mist our psyche.

It very well may be hard to clear your head when such a great amount of weight from the outside world is by all accounts pulling you down, yet is significantly progressively fundamental during these unpleasant stages throughout everyday life. When I began ruminating, another point of view on life conquered me. These are only a couple of proposals from an energetic tenderfoot that may enable somebody to start a remunerating routine with regards to reflection and mindfulness.

Checking through breaths, one practice that has helped me keep my brain in the ideal spot when reflecting is to check during breaths. As I breathe in, I check until I've finished breathing in, by and large around eight for me, yet can be anything relying upon how quick or moderate you tally. As I breathe out, I tally to a similar number, arriving at eight when I've finished my breath out. Rehashing this procedure, I tally to eight breathing in through my nose and after that considering to eight I breathe out through my mouth.

Cool air in/warm let some circulation into. I have likewise thought that it was gainful to focus on my breaths as cool, positive vitality filling my lungs and leaving as warm, negative vitality that has been stockpiled inside being discharged. Every breath is imagined, envisioning the positive, new cloud streaming in through my nose and pushing the negative, stale cloud out as I breathe out through my mouth.

Concentrate on a solitary item. Another training that can be utilized to encourage contemplation is to concentrate on a solitary article. The item can be anything. I most normally picture a solitary light lit in a dim live with nothing else around. I watch it glint as contemplations go through my brain, mindful of them however giving no consideration. As I get it, this sort of contemplation has really been utilized to help with recuperating explicit pieces of the body.

Use sound for ruminating. A bit much, yet something that has helped me out a lot, playing a sound can help with "timing " sessions, liberating me of considering to what extent I've been thinking. Here and there the utilization of sound can get you more profound, quicker, however, I have a houseful with five youngsters, so putting on earphones and covering up for twenty minutes is once in a while the main route for me to work on contemplating.

Practice each day. The increasingly more you accomplish something, the simpler and simpler it gets. This remains constant for reflection, as well. Doing it consistently builds up a sound propensity for taking a vital break and recognizing the present, excessively effectively overlooked with our bustling timetables in this day and age. Practice each day and see what opens up for you.

I'm still new to the act of reflection, so I comprehend the anxiety with newness. Be that as it may, I can't overlook the advantages of reflection as they are read and experience for myself, further supporting the idea we are in charge of our own condition. Also, as I proceed with my routine with regards to contemplation, I am charmingly astonished by the positive vitality I feel when setting aside the effort to find myself.

The Health Benefits of Energy Healing

It's extremely fascinating to take note of that dependent on a distributed American Heart Association's examination in November of 2012 about the effect of pressure decrease projects utilizing reflection the discoveries demonstrated that contemplation extraordinarily lessens stroke, cardiovascular failure, passing, outrage levels and the dangers related with coronary supply route illness.

The aftereffects of the program are very great with the members who contemplated two times per day for times of 20 minutes every day. They had the option to diminish coronary episode and stroke hazards by 48 percent. Furthermore, they likewise diminished their annoyance levels. It's intriguing to take note of that the more continuous the contemplation sessions, the higher the positive medical advantages for the members.

Adapting to consistent outrage is very damaging to the brain and body. There are sure things that one should relinquish, or leave if there's no desire for change. To refer to one model, poisonous connections are not just fatal; they are a hindrance to recuperating.

Chakra Meditation Music and Chakra Colors to Meditate

Music is another control that is additionally utilized in adjusting the chakras. Notwithstanding the music, the chief has included numerous wonderful and brilliant pictures. These chakra vitality hues are likewise a significant mending segment.

A case of chakra hues incorporates green which identifies with the substance and discharges genuinely stifled injury. Another powerful shading is indigo for the third eye that encourages us to see flawlessness no matter what. Blue is likewise utilized with throat chakra reflection and the declaration of truth through discourse.

Different methods used to help reflection incorporate guided symbolism, body unwinding, perception and breathing strategies. Regardless of whether you understand it or not, your Chakras are grinding away inside your body always. They impact your psychological just as your physical state. By giving extraordinary consideration to these zones, you can impact them to improve certain parts of your life.

Chapter 2 The 7 Chakras

You would often hear the word "chakra" when you are speaking with a spiritual healer, chiropractor, acupuncturist, or a yoga teacher. But, it's a word that's not commonly used in this modern world. In fact, the word "chakra" does not appeal to a lot of people because it sounds too "hippie" or "new age".

Many people think that these chakras are not real and that they do not exist. But, chakras are real and they have a huge impact in your life, whether you believe in them or not. They influence the level of your energy. They also govern your emotions, your health, and even the quality of your life and relationships.

But, what are chakras? Where are they located and why should you care about them?

Chakras are energy centers or fields of the body. These energy fields, primarily operate on your spirit or non-physical body, but they do correlate with areas of the physical body.

The chakras are wheels that move the energy up and down the body as they spin. They are connected to specific organs and glands in the body and they are responsible for the distribution of the life energy called "chi/qi" or "prana".

The chakras are the foundation of your energy ecosystem. Problems or deficiencies in this ecosystem can negatively affect the different areas of your life. When one or two of your chakras are blocked, you'd experience health and mental issues.

There are many energy centers in your body, but there are seven major chakras that are located from the base of your spine to the top of your head.

Solar Plexus Chakra (Manipura)

This chakra is located in the upper abdomen or the stomach area, between the rib and the navel. This chakra governs your self-confidence. It is associated with different organs such as the spleen, liver, small intestine, and pancreas.

People with balanced solar plexus chakra has a childlike energy. They are open-minded, stress free, and they respect authority. They have a strong sense of community and team spirit. They also have integrity and a strong will. They're also practical and intellectual.

The governing element of this chakra is fire. When this chakra is unbalanced, you'll have "gut feelings" that could make you feel stressed or agitated. You'll also have poor memory and concentration.

If you need a quick confidence booster, you have to take time to balance this chakra. Balancing this chakra makes you feel centered in spirit, body, and mind. It also helps you get more connected with your intuition or gut feelings so that you may act accordingly and with confidence.

This chakra is associated with various gems and stones, including malachite, topaz, and orange calcite.

Root Chakra (Mooladhara)

The root chakra is the first chakra and its color is red. It is the most dense of all the chakras. Its element is earth and located at the base of the spine, right above your tailbone.
This chakra is associated with bladder, kidneys, hips, legs, and the vertebral column.
This chakra is associated with different gems and stones such as fire agate, black tourmaline, blood stone, hematite, and tiger's eye.

Sacral Chakra (Swadhisthana)

The sacral chakra is the second chakra. It is located below the navel and above your pelvic bone. Its color is orange and is associated with various organs, including the uterus, prostate, testes, ovaries, intestines, belly, lower sacrum, and bladder.

People with balanced sacral chakra are generally enthusiastic, happy, energetic, sporty, self-assured, and constructive. When this chakra is balanced, your body moves freely and easily. You also enjoy good health. You are motivated and focused in pursuing your personal goals.

When you have a balanced sacral chakra, you interact harmoniously with others and you have happy and mutually supportive relationships. You'll feel fulfilled and you do not feel any void.

This chakra governs your ability to feel pleasure and enjoyment. It also influences your sexuality, desire, and libido. When your sacral chakra is balanced, you'll feel like a sex goddess or god. You'd be sexually confident and you have a satisfying sex life.

This chakra is associated with various gems and stones, including the citrine, carnelian, coral, and moonstone.

Heart Chakra (Anahata)

The heart chakra is the fourth chakra. It is located at the center of the chest. It is the center of the chakra system and it governs one's immune system, lungs, thymus glands, heart, and blood circulation. It also governs our ability to give and receive unconditional love.

People with balanced heart chakra are compassionate and caring. They also have the ability to easily adapt to change. They are calm, friendly, fun, and cheerful.

But, people with overactive heart chakra are codependent. They tend to be too concerned on the needs of other people, to the point of neglecting their own emotional needs. They love indiscriminately. This could lead to abuse and unhappiness.

People with unbalanced chakras are apathetic, unforgiving, hopeless, detached, distrustful, and detached. They also experience physical symptoms such as pneumonia, asthma, respiratory problems, upper back pain, and premature aging.

This chakra is associated with various gems and stones, including green jasper, emerald, jade, green tourmaline, rhodonite, green moldavite, dioptase, peridot, moss agate, aventurine, and chrysoprase.

Throat Chakra (Visuddha)

This chakra, as the name suggests, is located at the throat. It is associated with self-expression, creativity, and truth. This chakra allows you to communicate your thoughts and feelings. Its color is blue and its governing element is air.

When this chakra is balanced, you can easily express what you feel. You can easily communicate your beliefs, ideas, and emotions. You're also really creative – you sing, draw, write poetry, or do woodworking.

When your throat chakra is imbalanced, you'll most likely engage in habitual lying. So, if you have a habit of lying to yourself and others and you have a hard time separating lies from the truth, you may have an unbalanced throat chakra.

This chakra is associated with various gems and crystals including aquamarine, turquoise, lapis lazuli, and sodalite.

Third Eye Chakra (Ajna)

This chakra is located on the forehead, between the eyes. Its color is indigo and it represents our ability to see the big picture and make sound decisions.

When this chakra is not balanced, you easily feel stressed and your judgment is often clouded. You also have a hard time organizing your thoughts or making a practical decision.

This chakra is associated with different crystals and precious stones such as purple amethyst, tanzanite, danburite, satyaloka quartz, herderite, scolecite, petalite, and phenacite.

Crown Chakra (Sahasrara)

This chakra is located at the top of your head. It represents your spirituality and it allows you to experience pure bliss. It represents universal wisdom, inner peace, clarity, unity, and enlightenment. Its color is purple and its governing element is ether or space.

When this chakra is balanced, you have the ability to understand things in a much wider context. You feel that you are always in the right place at just the right time. You'll also feel empowered and joyful.

When this chakra is not balanced, you'd experience a number of psychological and physical issues such as depression, confusion, mental disconnection, schizophrenia, epilepsy, light sensitivity, headaches, and neurological disorders. Crown chakra imbalance also causes you to become selfish, greedy, materialistic, and domineering. So, if you're too bossy or you find joy in shopping at high end department stores, you may have an unbalanced crown chakra.

This chakra is associated with a number of crystals such as rainbow quartz, amethyst, black merlinite, beta quartz, hyalite opal, nirvana quartz, clear quartz, howlite, rutilated quartz, and sugilite.

The root chakra, solar plexus chakra, sacral chakra, heart chakra, throat chakra, third eye chakra, and the crown chakra are the seven major chakras. But, some chakra systems actually have 12 chakras, which include the earth star chakra, navel chakra, causal chakra, soul star chakra, and stellar gateway.

Soul Star
The eighth chakra is called the soul star chakra. This chakra cleanses and heals your lower body. It is located around eighteen inches above the crown chakra. This chakra is known as the seat of the soul. This chakra governs your life purpose.

Earth Chakra
The earth chakra is the ninth chakra. It is located one foot below the ground. This chakra keeps you connected to the earth. It is the center of a powerful force called Kundalini.

Solar Chakra
This is the tenth chakra. This chakra attaches you to the angels that dwell in the sun. This chakra plays an important role in spiritual evolution.

Galactic Chakra
This chakra is hooked up from the palm of your hand and it is linked into the galactic system.

So, if you want to get the best out of life, you should make an effort to clear your energy centers and make sure that they are functioning correctly.

How Chakras Work

We all have a physical body and we also have an energy body. Our energy body contains our auras and meridian lines. Auras are non-physical energy fields that surround a person. Your aura reveals your thoughts, dreams, and feelings. The colors of your aura may vary and they are usually seen by people who have special training in the healing arts.

A meridian line, on the other hand, is a path where the life energy called "qi" or "chi" passes through. It is typically used in Chinese medicine. If you go to an acupuncturist or a spiritual healer, you'll hear these terms often.

When you cut the body open, you won't see these auras and meridian lines, but you know that they are there. When you are familiar with auras, you'd know that they are affected by certain vibrations – good or bad. So, if you get a good vibe or bad vibe from someone, you may be feeling his aura. You get certain feelings when you talk with someone because these vibrations are contained in their energy.

Like the auras and meridian lines, the chakras are part of the body's energy anatomy. They operate as a ball of energy and they spin like a wheel to distribute your energy evenly throughout your body.

You can't see these chakras through an X-ray because they are not part of the physical body. They are part of our consciousness and they interact with the physical body through the different organs in the body. Each chakra is associated with one endocrine gland and a group of nerves called plexus.

Are some chakras more important than others? The answer is no. All chakras are equally important. To live a good life, you should balance all the chakras in your body.

The grounding function of the root chakra is just as important as the spiritual function of the crown chakra and the transcendent quality of the heart chakra.

To optimize your mental and bodily functions, you have to balance all your chakras and address your basic, relational, creative, safety, belongingness, and self-actualization needs.

The Chakras and Your Physical Body

We are all made of pure energy. So, if your energy centers are blocked, you'll experience various illnesses. When one or two of your chakras are not spinning, the energy is not evenly distributed throughout your body, resulting to some of the organs may not functioning well.

For example, your heart chakra is in your chest area and it covers the heart, and the respiratory system. So, if your heart chakra is not spinning, you'll experience heart and circulation problems. You are also susceptible to respiratory diseases and allergies.

The throat chakra governs the throat and mouth area of your body. So, if it's not functioning well, you'll experience mouth ulcers, sore throats, and thyroid problems.

Many Western medical practitioners do not believe this, but your chakras can affect your body functions. Balanced chakras can optimize your health and vitality while unbalanced chakras can wreak havoc in your life.

Chakras and Emotions

Chakras do not only represent your physical body, but also your emotions and parts of your consciousness. When there is tension in your consciousness, you'll feel it in the chakra that's linked to that part of your consciousness.

For example, if your boyfriend leaves you, you'll feel the pain in your heart or chest area. You'll feel like you can't breathe. When you are nervous about something, your bladder becomes weak and your legs tremble.

When the tension persists, it can result to physical symptoms.

The Chakras and The Quality of Life

The chakras do not only affect your physical body, they also affect your mental health and the overall quality of your life. So, if one part of your life seems off or something in your life is not working, then one of your chakras may be blocked.

When one or two of your chakras are blocked, some parts of your life may be doing well while other parts of your life may not be doing well at all. For example, your career may be doing well, but you have difficulty maintaining healthy relationships.

If you are a spiritual, kind, and compassionate person, but you have a hard time paying your bills, you may also have blocked chakras.

When your chakras are not functioning the way they should, you feel there is an imbalance. Your subconscious tells you that something is amiss.

The chakras represent who you are – your intellect, emotions, creativity, spirituality, sexuality, careers, principles and belief system. So, if your chakras are not balanced, you'll lose sight of one part of your life. You'll likely develop psychological problems such as depression, anxiety, delusions, and even nervous breakdown.

What Causes Chakra Blockages

Chakra blockages are caused by several factors – belief system, career, living situation, financial situation and relationships. Traumatic experiences such as abuse, accident, and loss of a loved one may also cause chakra blockages. Negative emotions such as anxiety, anger, stress, and fear may also put your chakras out of balance.

For example, being physically and emotionally abused by a former partner may cause heart chakra imbalance. You might have ended up closing yourself out to potential romantic partners. You may also tend to feel empty most of the time.

Your root chakra represents the foundation of your being. So, if your parents do not have enough money when you were growing up and they failed to provide enough for you, you'll most likely experience root chakra blockage. You may constantly fear that you do not have enough. You may also constantly worry about money.

Opening and Closing The Chakras

The opening and closing of your chakras work a lot like an energetic defense system. When you experience something traumatic or negative, the associated chakra will close itself to keep the negative energy out. If you are clinging to low frequency feelings such as anger, guilt, or blame, you'll experience chakra blockage.

Holding on to the following low frequency emotions for a long period can cause chakra blockage:

- Anger
- Pain
- Resentment
- Jealousy
- Covert hostility
- Grief
- Apathy
- Hopelessness

- Sadness
- Apathy
- Regret
- Pessimism
- Worry
- Blame
- Discouragement
- Shame
- Powerlessness
- Depression
- Disappointment
- Frustration
- Despair
- Guilt

The following positive or high frequency emotions can raise your vibrations and help open your chakras:

- Love
- Joy
- Acceptance
- Eagerness
- Optimism

- Passion
- Hopefulness
- Contentment
- Faith
- Belief

So, to keep your chakras balanced, you must let go of egoism. You must choose to act with love.

Chakras and Empaths

Many people have open chakras. These people are called empaths. They are highly sensitive people. They easily pick up other people's energy so they find public places overwhelming. They also know when someone is not being honest with them. They are creative and they have a strong need for solitude. They feel weak when they are exposed to toxic people.

Empaths should keep their chakras guarded and balanced. They should carry protective stones such as rose quartz, black tourmaline, amethyst, and malachite. These stones help balance emotions and remove anxieties and negative energy.

Chapter 3 Identifying Blocked Chakras

Now that you have a little bit better idea of what the chakras are and why they are so important, it is time to move on to what the different chakras are all about. Each chakra is going to take care of a different part of your wellbeing, but they all do work together to make you happy and healthy overall. When one of the chakras is not working the way that it should, you are going to start to notice, over time, how the other ones are going to start going down as well. Let's take a look at some of the different chakras in the body and how each of them will be able to work in your body.

Let's start at the top of the body and work our way down, explaining where the chakras are located and what they represent. The Crown Chakra is possibly one of the most important since it is located at the top of the head and is linked to the way you connect to life in a spiritual way. If you are feeling out of sorts and at loggerheads with the world, then this chakra is one that is perhaps blocked and needs to be freed up to allow you to gain the most that you can from your life. Your connection with the universe and your ability to feel calm within it is affected by this Chakra.

The Third Eye Chakra is located centrally on your forehead, and you may have heard tales about people who can see what others are unable to. This area accounts for things such as second sight and the ability to see beyond the normal. That can include gifts such as telepathy but is not limited to such. If the Third Eye Chakra is opened, you are able to have a greater understanding or achieve enlightenment. Buddhist monks who concentrate on perfecting their meditation are trying to achieve that enlightenment.

The Throat Chakra is an important one. Have you ever felt stressed? If you have, then the chances are that your neck hurts. This point in your body is susceptible to pain, but it's much more than that. It signifies your ability to communicate with others and to be able to express yourself. If you are shy or if you find that you have self-esteem issues, then the chances are that this chakra will be blocked.

If you were to imagine the area of the heart, you would instantly associate this with the emotional feeling of love – and you wouldn't be too far removed from what the heart chakra is all about. The heart chakra is located in the center of your chest, a little higher than the heart, and is responsible for your ability to love unconditionally. It is through this chakra that people are able to feel an inner sense of peace. Thus, if you are stressed or your life is problematic, perhaps this chakra needs more attention.

Have you ever had problems breathing, digestive problems or simply that feeling that you have a knot in your stomach? Most people have at some stage of their lives. The Solar Plexus chakra is located in the upper abdomen of the stomach. This accounts for many of those feelings of insecurity. For example, you may not feel a sense of self-worth, or you may feel at odds with the world. That's not uncommon.

Kate was one client who came to me with problems of this nature. By teaching her exercises to open up this area and allow energy to flow, she was able to overcome her insecurity. You won't mend this area right away, but yoga poses will help. Most of the time, this Chakra is affected by lifestyle choices and also the way we feel about ourselves, and that has to be dealt with in conjunction with exercises. In Kate's case, she was taught to breathe correctly, and this helped to rectify the problems.

The Sacral Chakra is also one that may affect your sense of well-being, insofar as your sexuality is concerned. This is found two inches above your navel. It also affects the way you feel about what you get back out of life, or your sense of abundance.

What about feeling grounded? This is dealt with by the chakra at the base of the spine. This Chakra – known as the Root Chakra is the chakra that affects how you feel about your life, your sense of security, your earnings and ability to look after yourself. Your independence is also affected by this Chakra.

They are important and can make a big difference in the way you live your life. When you feel any kind of discomfort, try to imagine the chakra that may be blocking energy and work on that particular chakra until you notice an improvement. We have given you all the information you need to do this. Be the person you were intended to be and find happiness and fulfillment by taking the right road toward enlightenment. You will find your life will improve beyond measure when you are able to do this.

Chapter 4 The Planets and Your Chakras

Like how every chakra has an associated endocrine system gland, every chakra has a planet associated with it. There are ruling planets, all of which have a specific nature and set of characteristics. The chakras also have similar characteristics. Most often, the planets are used in relation to your birthdate and time. The specific planetary alignment when you were born can influence and determine who you are as a person. This alignment and relationship are captured in a birth chart. What is interesting about your birth chart is that it does not only tell you about your mental, spiritual, and physical aspects, it also illustrates the power your planetary alignment has over your energy and chakras. When you took your first breath, you drew in the energy of the Universe at that moment, making a lasting impression on every cell in your body. That stamp is a permanent part of who you are. That moment that defined your existence, it also defined your calling. You are meant to bring that gift back to those around you throughout your entire life.

One way to think about your chakra system in terms of the planets is that your chakra system is a reflection of the solar system. You are essentially a "microcosm of the macrocosm." In that sense, you contain all the energy stored in the Universe inside yourself.

Your Root Chakra

Also known as your Mooladhara, the chakra located at the base of your spine is ruled by the planet Mars. Linked with the astrological sign Aries, this planet is related to innocence, connection to the Earth, directional sense, wisdom, joy, and purity. Your actions are decisive, wise, and aligned with the correct direction of your purpose. You have a beautiful ability to always make the "right" decision. Your actions are strong and you are powerful, but in a way that is kind and friendly. Mars' energy, and therefore, the energy of your Root chakra, is instinctual, natural, and intense. You are courageous and dynamic, as well as very physical. If this planet and chakra is strong for you, you often have a childlike innocence about you and a love for "discovering" life.

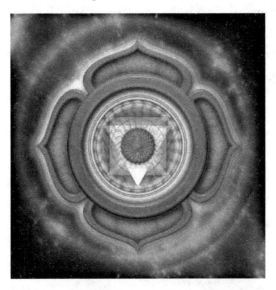

This planet and chakra are connected to your sexuality. If there is an imbalance or poorly affected planet, your sexuality can go to the extreme. In addition, this energy is responsible for your reproduction and associated organs. If you have extreme encounters and non-innocent behaviors related to these organs, you can harm their sensitivity. The stronger this alignment and clarity in this center, the purer you feel. Also, the stronger the alignment, you are more emboldened to live according to your purpose and purity.

Your Sacral Chakra

Also called your Swadisthan, this chakra is related to the planet Mercury. It is located in your lower abdomen area and Mercury governs over the astrological signs Virgo and Gemini. This chakra and planet are responsible for your digestion. You break down fat cells and send them into your body for energy. This process is necessary for the proper function of your brain. Because it supplies the energy to the brain, it also strengthens your ability to comprehend and think about things. Creativity and a sense of beauty are also connected to this energy. Influential Mercury can help you find a practical solution for various problems that are comprehensible and wise. This is because of the wisdom and creativity housed in both this chakra and its ruling planet.

Mercury is known for being a bridge between the mind, physical body, and the soul. The pure knowledge of the Universe enters your body from this location. The sciences and the fine arts flow from here. This is because you are able to grasp the most complicated concepts and solve problems in a clear and creative manner. If you have a strong influence from Mercury, you are always "in your head." While this is great for solving problems, it can be troublesome with relationships. You can become impatient and angry easily. It is important to balance your second chakra to help level out this mental state and the corresponding emotions. Continue making clearly understood and honest decisions.

Your Solar Plexus Chakra

Sometimes also called your Nabhi, this chakra is located in your lower diaphragm or stomach area. It is associated with the characteristics of evolution, generosity, morality, balance, and satisfaction. It is also strong with self-acceptance and acceptance of others. The same traits apply its governing planet, Jupiter. This planet also governs the astrological sign, Sagittarius. The nature of this planet is helpful and generous, but it also can cause everything to be prosperous or increase. This can be great when it is applied to good things but challenging when it enhances the bad. It is also associated with "good luck," so you have a better chance of a good outcome. This is especially true when considering your finances, which are related to this chakra and planet. It supports both your spiritual well-being and your mental state.

When it is a positive influence on your life, you are thankful for what you already have and able to easily share it with others when you see they are in need. You are a very generous person. This means that as your "luck" increases and more wealth comes to you, you are then able and willing to spread that wealth out to others. You never worry about being provided for; you are sure that the Universe will continue to give you all the support you need. You never feel the need to ask for more than you are given.

If your influence is harmed or negative, you may suffer from indecision or a significant imbalance. Your thinking can become extreme and fanatical. Because everything is heightened with this energy, you can become tyrannical and fanatical. You could rake in debt without clear thought, all to seek luxury and beautiful things. This is why balance is so important. The planet Jupiter rules over your philosophy, religion, sense of honesty, and justice. When you are born with this planet's positive influence, you are naturally honest, virtuous, and moral. As you grow, this influence also enhances, making you more connected to your virtues and have a bigger sense of justice. It is also likely that you will continue throughout your life to try to "better" yourself and offer healing and guidance to others around you to be able to do the same.

Your Heart Chakra

This chakra houses your soul, which is pure, untainted, unconditional love. This is why this chakra is associated with compassion, pure love, and self-confidence. It is also a chakra of detachment. Great parents are developed from a strong and open Heart chakra. The planet which governs this space in your body is Venus, which also governs the astrological signs Libra and Taurus. A good influence and well-functioning Venus nature make others around you feel "good." You create beauty and balance around you.

It is likely that if you have Venus in your birth chart that you are very beautiful. This beauty is more than a surface attraction, as it runs deep inside of you. Your attitude and behaviors are reflected, showing others your inner love and confidence. You help others transform their lives through your own positivity, sweetness, and kindness. The more open your Heart chakra, the more connected to your Soul you become. And the more open your Heart, the more your unconditional love spreads to everything around you. This love then sparks the Heart of others, encouraging them to open their Hearts as well.

Your Throat Chakra

Your Vishuddhi, or your fifth chakra, is where you are able to feel the connection as part of the Universe. You are a piece of everything; the Earth, other people, the Universe, and all the elements. Saturn is the ruling planet for this chakra. Saturn is the planet governing the astrological signs, Aquarius and Capricorn. The hard part about this planet in your birth chart is the deep loneliness you can feel. It is a planet for teachers, but a well-disciplined teacher is distant and kind. And like a disciplined teacher, Saturn sends you tests to help strengthen your characteristics, especially your weakest ones. It will unveil the part of your character that needs most work and offer the opportunity to develop it. This means situations can appear useless, limited, or full of unnecessary obstacles. Keep in mind this happens so you can learn something valuable and grow. Once you recognize your limitations, you are then offered the opportunity to detach, find firm ground, and be stable.

In addition, Saturn and your Throat chakra help you identify the difference between something that is "wrong" or "right." This includes things going on inside your body. You can rely on this ability when you are being tested. You will be able to trust that you know the right from the wrong in a situation because of this open chakra. Often, because of the detachment, you are a great and fair "witness" of life. You can enjoy life while you fulfill your purpose, and not attach to the drama, challenges, or tragedies of life. You can watch life unfold as if a play on a stage and you can enjoy what you see without feeling attached to the scenes and characters.

If this chakra is blocked or Saturn is not functioning properly in your life, you can become very pessimistic. It can become hard for you to see the good in people and situations. You will also have a tendency to feel sorry for yourself and assume a "victim mentality." You can feel full of woes and hardships, without looking to find the lessons in the situations.

Your Third Eye Chakra

Agnya, your sixth chakra, is situated in the middle of your forehead. Your conditioning and ego sit here. The Sun is the ruling planet for this chakra. The Sun governs your sense of being and your character. It is related to the energy the Sun is located in. This means your main sign or planet. Wherever it is located, you can learn about the stage of your own evolution. It reveals where you are in the process towards enlightenment or true understanding, as well as illuminate the lessons you need to learn in this lifetime. Your identity is formed in this chakra and with this planet. There are many facets to your identity and "who" you are. That is how you are a truly unique soul. Influences on your identity include your community you choose to engage in, the way you view the world, friends, education, family, etc. The challenge is that these identities are all developed through your Ego.

Your Ego is conditioning. When your Third Eye is open, your Ego cannot rule. This is because your Soul is able to expand, revealing your true identity. As you recognize your True Self, you become humbler. If the Sun is too domineering in your birth chart, you may struggle with your ego. You will be more egotistical, conceited, and dominating than necessary. You may also be vain. This vanity can block your sixth chakra from operating properly. You may develop a sense of superiority, disconnecting you from those around you and from your Source. You do not reveal your True Self because you are operating and being ruled by Ego. When you open it and connect with your Soul, you have an amazing way to forgive. You feel connected to your Self and everything else around you, knowing that what lies within you also lies within them.

Your Crown Chakra

The last major chakra is your Sahasrara, or Crown Chakra. This sits on the top or just above the center of your skull, on the top of your head. When you were a baby, this is where there is a soft spot; the place where the skull bones had not hardened and closed over yet. The Moon is the ruling planet for this chakra. The moon also rules over the astrological sign, Cancer. This chakra sits above all others and is actually the culmination and combination of all the other chakras combined. All the energy and traits of the various chakras converge at this point. The governance of the Moon includes your mind, instincts, and emotions. When you open or have a flowing Crown chakra, all the other chakras have an easier time working together. It also helps you connect with the energy of the Universe. This deep connection moves you past just your consciousness. The Moon in your birth chart symbolizes the space beyond consciousness and is an always existing state. It controls the entire Universe.

This means when your Crown is open and flowing, your consciousness is connected to the Universe's intelligence or consciousness. If you have a strong Moon presence in your birth chart, you are spiritual, sacrificing, creative, instinctive, and sensitive. The Moon is feminine and productive. It represents and develops the sense of being a mother or nurturing to others.

The Moon circles the zodiac faster than any other planet, meaning the nature of the Moon is constantly changing. This change causes a change in your personality. This is a constant current in your life; change. This means you have a strong ability to adapt quickly and easily to most changes. This is beneficial to you because the Universe is also always changing. When you have a strong connection to the Moon and this chakra is open, you feel like a single drop mixed seamlessly into the whole of the ocean, ebbing and flowing with harmony amongst the collective as the collective.

Chapter 5 Balancing and Healing The Chakras

Chakras are centers of energy and power that take in energy and distribute it throughout the body. The chakras are continuously affected by the way that people interact with different situations in life and with different people in different places on an emotional, mental, and/or physical level. The chakra both collects and absorbs energy. Chakras can be thought of as the medium through which the body is nourished with balance and health, or they can deplete a person's well-being, health, and vitality. It all depends on how that person lives their individual life.

As long as a person is in a state of deep relaxation, whether during meditation or while asleep, then the intelligence that exists in the forces of life will flow easily through the chakras. When people are awake they are dominated by their ego-mind and their self-conscious biological life force. The ego-mind creates stress and conflict that causes the life force to suffer damage during waking hours where it had been healing during states of altered consciousness like the ones experienced during asleep. The mind is probably the largest stumbling block that prevents energy from flowing freely through the body.

It is on the emotional and mental level that most of the health issues suffered by people are created. These issues appear in the body as blocks that are psychosomatic in nature. The system of chakras in the body is aligned with the endocrine glands and the nerve centers in the body, a replica of energy on a level that is very subtle. Chakras are not physical entities in the human body but rather are tied to the psychic centers of the mind and the neurological centers of the body.

Inner stress and conflict are created by the unresolved traumatic experiences that humans experience during life. Blocked energy in the chakras is caused by emotional, mental, and physical health problems. It is fundamental to overall good health to remove energy blocks and clean and balance the chakras. This will also help to alleviate and eliminate the feeling that one is stuck in the overwhelming instances of past experiences that cause illness, disharmony, and stress. Since people can't feel the energy of the chakras radiating through the body it is easy to dismiss this power as non-existent or not really relevant. But conflict and disturbances that are felt on the emotional, mental, and physical level convert biological energy into subconscious fate. In other words, the pains that are suffered physically and emotionally become the ideas by which the body is driven, such as "I have felt suffering and now my body must feel suffering". Living with unbalanced chakras is the basic source of all the suffering that humans endure.

When the chakras are out of balance, especially the first three, the self will go in search of things to acquire from the external world. When the energy of the chakras is sent out from the body instead of being held in to fuel the body, then negative emotions such as loneliness, despair, depression, and fear take over the mind. These are the negative emotions that will have a negative effect on the physical well-being of the body. So the body begins to search externally for things to make it feel better, things like work, relationships, food, drugs, alcohol, and sex. While these are temporary pain relievers they must continuously be fed into the body and the body will continuously crave more and greater amounts. This is where the addiction begins.

The chakras will become healed and balanced when one takes the time to step away from bad habit patterns and those behaviors that create internal conflicts and learn to be aware of the self and the world instinctively. That is, to not necessarily choose certain things but to accept what comes. When the power of the mind is not allowed to dominate the innate wisdom of the body, then healing and balancing will happen. Behavior that is self-destructive caused energy to flow down through the body and out into the world, instead of flowing up through the chakras to the Crown Chakra to give a better connection to the spiritual world.

There are many different methods that can and should be used to balance the chakras. Yoga is one of these methods. Yoga is not just about standing or lying in a certain position until the time limit is up. Yoga is more of a way of life, a lifestyle to be developed and nurtured for optimum chakra health and well-being. The traditions and the teachings of yoga offer specific techniques that, when used correctly, will restore the power of balance to the chakras. These methods include working with the breath; poses and exercise; learning how not to react negatively to emotions, actions, and thoughts; visualizing; chanting and mantras, and meditating.

Over the last several thousand years' yogis have experimented with, studied, and learned from the power of breathing and how to use breath as a method to restore balance to the chakras and restore peace to the mind. As a method used to withdraw from patterns of behavior that create conflict and self-destructive habit, breath is a very powerful tool. Proper breathing will reverse the flow of energy from a downward flow into an upward flow that will assist in feeding the higher chakras. This, in turn, will help eliminate the patterns of bad habits that consume and eventually destroy life.

When the breath comes into the left side of the nose it is the representative of the Moon and it is cooling to the right side of the brain. The breath that comes into the right side of the nose represents the Sun and it is warming to the left side of the brain. Using the technique of alternate nostril breathing is a good way to bring harmony to the chakras as well as the spirit, body, and the mind by bringing balance to the breath. This technique works to calm the mind. It also allows energy to freely move throughout the body. This will naturally give power to the body to enable it to use its own healing abilities that nature gave it.

To use this breath technique, sit down in a position that is comfortable. With closed eyes become aware of the breath itself. Put total awareness onto the breath itself. Become aware of the very top part of the head where the Crown Chakra will be located. Imagine a golden light like strong early morning sunlight radiating onto the Crown Chakra and down into the body. This bright light flows into the body and down the spine. Every incoming breath brings love, energy, vitality, and life. As the light finally reaches the bottom of the spine imagine it collecting in a great pool, like a lake of golden sunshine at the base of the spine. Now exhale and allow the breath to pull up some of the golden glowing sunshine through the body, out through the arms and the top of the head, lighting the entire top half of the body. Push out all negativity and any other emotions that are not needed with the exhale. When this exercise is down consciously and slowly it will bring the energy of life into the body. This technique can be used for just a few minutes or it can be used to enter a deeper state of meditation and relaxation.

Exercises and yoga poses are necessary for properly balancing the chakras. As a method for balancing the chakras, yoga is one of the most basic. It works by creating alignment in the physical part of the body. Yoga poses use stabilizing and balancing methods to restore the physical balance to the human body. Returning physical balance to the body will work to rebalance the position of the chakras in the body and help toward rebalancing them. The poses that specifically work for balancing the chakras are sometimes referred to as chakra yoga. The poses are specifically designed to keep the body straight and aligned along the spinal column so that the path for the flow of energy from one chakra to the next remains straight and strong.

The poses done in yoga are an amazing way to balance and cleanse the chakras. The strengthening and stretching will benefit the health of the body which will, in turn, lead to better overall health in the mind and the spirit.

The yoga method known as Kundalini yoga is the one thought of when considering ways to use yoga to balance the chakras. Kundalini yoga blends the spiritual and the technical aspects of yoga in an effort to achieve chakra balance. Also sometimes known in practice as the yoga of awareness, it mixes postures, meditation, and breathing exercises to bring balance and harmony to the chakras. It is also the method used to awaken the Kundalini energy, which is a strong life force that is housed at the end of the spine near the Root Chakra. The main goal of this method is to send the energy from the Root Chakra through the other chakras. The method begins with awakening the Kundalini in the Root Chakra and using that energy to activate all of the other chakras upward along the spine until the Crown Chakra is reached. Then the chakra circuit is considered to be complete and true enlightenment is attainable.

Using affirmations is another way to balance and heal the chakras. An affirmation is nothing more than a statement of positivity and empowerment that is used for one of many different purposes. Affirmations are particularly helpful when balancing and healing the chakras. Using an affirmation often has an immediate positive effect on the person's personal vibration and overall mood. The powerful words that are used to create the affirmation itself are used to empower the spirit, reprogram the mind, and heal the body. Using affirmations to heal and balance the chakras will help a person to work toward achieving a goal, have the power to remain motivated, and be able to create positive changes that are long-lasting in the life.

An affirmation works by replacing purposefully any limiting or negative beliefs, ideas, or thoughts that have been stored internally over the years. These thoughts will be replaced with new statements that are positive and assertive that outline how life should be experienced and how life should be lived for a more positive lifestyle. Regularly using affirmations with the intention that is focused on the affirmation will work to heal and balance the complete system of chakras and will help to transform life in ever more amazing ways.

Making dietary changes is a great idea when deciding to heal and balance the chakras. Everyone has those moments where they feel emotional, frustrated, anxious, depressed, exhausted, and unsuccessful. But there is a way to remove those feelings from being a regular part of everyday life and return to the motivated awesome people hidden deep inside. Everyone has heard of the theory of eating the rainbow. The philosophy of Ayurveda takes eating the rainbow to an entirely new level. With this philosophy, the goal is to eat certain colors of foods in order to emotionally realign the mind through eating foods that are good for the body.

Using Reiki is another way to balance and heal the chakras. Reiki is the Higher Intelligence that is used to guide the entire universe, from creation to daily function. This wisdom of Rei subtly guides humans in times of need and also acts as a way to guide everyday life. Its nature is infinite so therefore it is all-knowing. Ki is what is known as the energy that is non-physical that is used to provide animation to life forms. If Ki is high in a person then they will feel confident and strong. They will be more than capable of taking on the challenges of life and enjoying life to the fullest. If the Ki in the body is low, then the person is more likely to become sick and feel physically weak. Ki comes from sleeping, air, sunshine, and food.

So Reiki is a healing energy that is not physical and is made up of the force of life of energy that is naturally guided by a person's spirituality. Reiki cannot be guided by the mind so it is not subject to being guided by the ability or the experience of the person who is using it. It is also not able to be misused because it will always create and affect that is healing and balancing.

The human mind lives not just in the brain but also in the body. It is also located in the aura of the person. This is because the thoughts of the mind create physical reactions in the body. Ki will be found to be restricted at those places where negative feelings and thoughts are collected in the body. If Ki is restricted around a physical organ it means that the organ is not working the way that it could be to be functioning at maximum ability. When the mind is not able to eliminate negative feelings and thoughts quickly and they are allowed to be stored as physical manifestations in the body then illnesses take over.

The best point about Reiki is that it is not guided by humans but by a Higher Power. When Reiki is allowed to follow its own instinctive course then it will know where to go to and know how to respond to any restrictions it finds in the body. Reiki will work in the mind and the body in the unconscious parts and will work directly on negative feelings and thoughts to allow the normal flow of goodness to return.

Each individual chakra also has a corresponding crystal and a stone. The crystals will help to heal the chakra and the stones are used to keep the chakra in balance. The results in using the crystals and the stones provide effects that can be felt profoundly on a spiritual, emotional, and physical level. If chakras are unhealthy or unbalanced then the mind, spirit, and the body cannot properly function. Using crystals and stones to balance and heal the chakras will effectively and easily return the person to an overall healthy and vibrant balance of energy.

There are so many different methods available to balance the chakras and return them to their healthy function that it makes absolutely no sense to continue on a path of illness, dysfunction, or any of the other negative thoughts and emotions that are associated with having blocked chakras. Explore the different ways to unblock, balance, and heal the chakras. Choose one or several methods to try. It is better to use more than one method because they all work together to achieve the goal of healthy chakra. And when the chakras are aligned, open, healthy, and balanced then life will be much more worth living.

Chapter 6 Ways to Heal and Balance The Chakras

You have now understood the techniques to heal and balance your chakras. This chapter will deal with the healing and balancing of individual chakras. If you know that any specific chakra in your body is not functioning properly, you can take the following steps to clear the blockage in the chakra and also balance the energy flow.

This chapter will not only tell you about the specific tools to heal the chakras but will also suggest some important lifestyle and behavioral changes. By incorporating these changes, you can expect faster healing and a greater balance in life and your energies. You'll find that controlling your mind and emotions would become easier and it'd be easy to remain stress-free and happy.

Root Chakra Healing

Lifestyle Changes

- Practice Earth Sitting and Hiking

To balance the root chakra, it is very important that you establish a close connection with the earth as the physical element of this chakra is earth. You may feel ungrounded when this chakra gets blocked or out of balance. Try to be as close to the earth for some time every day. Earth Sitting is a good way to establish a connection with the earth. You can also go for hiking trips as that also connects you with the earth.

- Do Gardening

Gardening is another way to establish a deep connection with the earth. Every plant that you handle while gardening has its roots deep inside the earth. You get to establish a direct connection with the roots. You also need to handle a lot of earth in the process of gardening, and that also helps in restoring the balance.

- Increase Physical Activity

Imbalance in this chakra can make you inactive. Excessive and sudden weight gain is one of the side-effects of imbalance in the root chakra. To restore the balance, it is important that you incorporate a lot of physical activity in your life. If your work involves intense physical work, then it's ok; otherwise, join a gym. Sweating every day is very important to bring a balance. If you are trying to restore the balance in your root chakra while leading a sedentary lifestyle, you are up for a great challenge.

- Try Walking Barefoot in Grass

Waling barefoot in the grass in gardens is another way to establish a sensory connection with this earth. It is a very soothing and relaxing exercise. There are several other health benefits of this activity too. However, it is very good for healing the root chakra. After the walks, you'll feel more grounded, rational, and secure.

- Eat Red Fruits

RED IS THE COLOR OF THIS CHAKRA. EATING RED FRUITS AND KEEPING RED THINGS AROUND YOU WILL HELP YOU IN HEALING THIS CHAKRA FASTER.

Yoga Asanas

There are several important yoga asanas that can help in faster healing and balancing of this chakra. Some of them are:

- Standing Forward Bend
- Head-to-Knee pose
- Supported Corpse Pose
- Warrior I
- Warrior II
- Tree pose

- Chair pose
- Supported Child's pose

Meditation

Meditation is an excellent way to heal and balance the chakras. You should focus on the pelvic region while you meditate and try to connect it with your third eye chakra. Try to expand and contract this region consciously, and that would also help in stimulating the energies in this chakra.

Crystals

Black tourmaline, bloodstone, hematite, obsidian, ruby, garnet, onyx, lodestone, fire agate, red jasper, and smoky quartz can be really helpful in restoring the balance in this chakra.

Essential Oils
Myrrh, patchouli, sandalwood, and spikenard are some of the essential oils that are effective in healing the root chakra.

Sacral Chakra Healing

Lifestyle Changes
- Give Proper Vent to Your Sexual Energy

This chakra is highly bent toward enjoying the bounties of this world. The physical location of this chakra is very close to your genitals, and hence, the sexual energy in your body can become unbalanced easily. It is important that you give proper vent to your sexual energy. If your sexual energy is not getting the proper expression, you may develop negativity. Your temperament may change, and your social behavior can become aggressive. It is important for you to have a balanced and active sexual life to keep this chakra in sync.

- Explore New Things

This chakra likes to explore new things. However, if the energies in this chakra are out of balance, you may show a lack of interest in everything. The easy way to restore the balance is to force yourself to do new things. Try new food, clothes, and places. Change and variety will help in healing the chakras faster.

- Try Creative Pursuits

This chakra has a high potential to be creative. This is the chakra of the explorers. It has great creative energy trapped inside. If you try new and creative things, it can help in stimulating the energy centers of this chakra.

- Get Involved in Community Service

This chakra likes to live for itself, but this can also make a person self-serving, overindulgent, and indifferent. All these things can lead to imbalance. To keep your sacral chakra in balance, you must get involved with some kind of community service.

- Take Help of Reiki Healing

Reiki healing is a terrific way to find the blockages in this chakra and resolve them. If you have developed distaste for everything all of a sudden, you must consult a reiki healer immediately for help.

- Orange Color

THE COLOR OF THIS CHAKRA IS ORANGE. IT IS ONE OF THE MOST VIBRANT AND FLAMBOYANT COLORS. IT GIVES YOU A DISTINCT FLAVOR AND PERSONALITY. IF THIS CHAKRA IS OUT OF BALANCE, EATING ORANGE COLOR FRUITS AND KEEPING THE THINGS OF THIS COLOR NEAR YOU CAN HELP IN RESTORING THE ENERGY BALANCE.

Yoga Asanas

Some of the important yoga asanas for healing chakra imbalance are:

- Happy baby pose
- Child's pose
- Downward facing dog
- Cow face pose
- Bound angle pose
- Open-angle pose
- Warrior poses
- Four limb staff pose

Meditation

You must focus on the area just below your navel when you meditate. Try to feel the orange light there. Inculcate positive thoughts and let go of the repressed memories and emotions.

Crystals

Orange tourmaline, sunstone, carnelian, moonstone, and amber are some of the crystals that can help in healing this chakra.

Essential Oils

Patchouli, rosewood, sandalwood, and ylang-ylang are some of the important essential oils that can be used to treat the imbalance in this chakra.

Solar Plexus Chakra Healing

Lifestyle Changes
- Practice healthy boundaries

Imbalance in this chakra may make you forget personal and professional boundaries. The best way to balance this chakra is to start practicing healthy boundaries in your personal as well as professional lives. Don't try to encroach the space of others. The more you follow the boundaries, the easier it would get to lead a healthy life. Your solar plexus chakra will also start settling down if you bring down the aggressive and encroaching tendencies.

- Sun gazing

This chakra gets its power from the sun and also illuminates inside you like a sun. If you are feeling low in energy in this chakra or you are not able to focus on your projects, try sun gazing early in the morning at the time of dawn when the sun is crimson red. It will give power to your chakra.

- *Sunbathing*

In the same way as sun gazing, sunbathing is also equally beneficial for treating the imbalance in the solar plexus chakra. It will also help you in getting rid of several skin issues.

- Physically active routine

It is very important that to keep this chakra energized, you maintain a physically active routine. This chakra doesn't work well in the people who are leading a very sedentary lifestyle. This is the chakra of the hardworking lot. Try to get involved in some job that requires intense physical work or devote some time in the gym or play outdoor sports.

- Breaking the comfort zone

This is a chakra that sets new norms. It makes you try harder and excel in everything you do. If you adopt a lifestyle in which you don't want to come out of your comfort zone and take new challenges, this chakra will get out of balance. To keep this chakra active, keep taking new challenges. Come out of your comfort zone and do things that you haven't tried before.

- *Yellow*

YELLOW IS THE COLOR OF THIS CHAKRA, AND HENCE, YELLOW-COLORED FRUITS AND THINGS IN THIS COLOR

WILL BE BENEFICIAL FOR RESTORING THE ENERGY BALANCE IN THIS CHAKRA.

Yoga Asanas

Some of the important yoga asanas for healing chakra imbalance are:

- Pranayam or breathing techniques
- Bellows breath
- Boat pose
- Half-boat pose
- Sun salutation
- Cat pose
- Cow pose

Meditation

You can practice body scan meditation and various breathing meditations for healing this chakra. These meditation techniques help in feeling the raw power in your body, and you are able to get hold of your physicality much better.

Crystals

Yellow Citrine, yellow topaz, yellow tiger's eye, amber, rutilated quartz, and yellow agate can be very helpful crystals for healing the energy imbalance in this chakra.

Essential Oils

Rosewood, lemon, lavender, roman chamomile, and rosemary are some of the important essential oils for healing the imbalance in this chakra.

Heart Chakra Healing

Lifestyle Changes

- Learn new art forms

The heart chakra is the center of creation. If this chakra is out of balance, the best way to restore energy balance is to ignite the creative spark in you. Try to learn some new creative art form. Listen to music, learn to play musical instruments, drawing, painting, singing, dancing, and all other creative ways to express your energies can help you in stimulating the energy center in this chakra.

- Treat yourself well

This chakra can be out of balance if you are not getting due attention or care. Emotional stability is very important for this chakra as it is very sensitive in nature. To restore the balance, you must indulge yourself in self-care. Treat yourself frequently. Give yourself enough of 'me time.' Don't ignore your needs for long. Repressed emotions can have a very negative impact on this chakra's energy balance.

- Love someone

This chakra has a deep longing for love. Whenever there is an imbalance in this chakra, people start feeling unloved, undesired, and unwanted. To keep this chakra in balance, love someone. It isn't important to love a person in particular. Invest your love into anything. Love pets, art forms, passions, or people around you.

- Remain motivated

You need to keep yourself motivated to keep this chakra in balance. Negativity, depression, and regret are some of the emotions that can trip the balance of this chakra. Listen to motivational talks and indulge yourself in activities that invoke optimism. Your positive attitude can help a lot in keeping this chakra balanced.

- Do charity or social work

Charity or social work are also great ways to keep this chakra working smoothly. The more you work for others, the more you become receptive of positive energies. You become accepting in nature. This is a great way to keep the heart chakra in balance.

- Go in the wild

Spending time in the wild is a great way to give your heart chakra a boost. Nature has a great healing impact on the heart chakra. It restores the positive balance in the body. You should take frequent breaks from your routine life and go back to the lap of nature.

- Accept new people

This chakra works best when you are accepting in nature. Do not have rigid ideas in your mind about people. Be more accepting and embracing. Accept people for who they are without attaching qualifications. This can help you in keeping the balance in the chakra intact.

- *Green*

THE COLOR OF THIS CHAKRA IS GREEN. EATING GREEN FRUITS AND VEGETABLES AND KEEPING GREEN COLOR AROUND YOU WILL HELP IN HEALING THIS CHAKRA FASTER.

Yoga Asanas

Some of the important yoga asanas for healing chakra imbalance are:

- Eagle pose
- Arm balances
- Camel pose
- Seated spinal twist

Meditation

A guided meditation that helps you in becoming embracing in nature is the best for restoring the balance in this chakra. Loving and kindness meditation is one of the best ways to heal this chakra. You must keep your mind filled with sweet emotions when you work on this chakra. You shouldn't form too many ideas in your mind as this chakra can make you imagine weird things.

Crystals

Rose quartz, jade, green calcite, emerald, green kyanite, and green tourmaline are some crystals that can help in healing and balancing this chakra.

Essential Oils

Ylang-ylang, rose, palmarosa, bergamot, geranium, neroli, lavender, and melissa are some important essential oils that can be used to heal the imbalance in this chakra.

Throat Chakra Healing

Lifestyle Changes

- Don't lie

This is the first chakra that takes you on the path of intellectual and spiritual awakening. It is also a chakra that has a lot of power vested in the throat. If you lie a lot, the throat chakra will get affected. This chakra doesn't support lying. You will not only start losing the power in your voice, but you may also start having mental clarity issues. The most important way to restore the energy balance in this chakra is to stop lying in your day to day life.

- Develop the habit of discussion

The more you will discuss things with others, the greater will be the influence of this chakra. Discussions with people help this chakra in becoming more expressive. Do not keep your thoughts to yourself. Indulge yourself in healthy discussions with wise people. You will find that your mental clarity would increase and the impact of throat chakra would also become visible.

- Work on the art of public speaking

Public speaking is the forte of the throat chakra. A person who has the energies centered in the throat chakra will be a great orator. However, if your throat chakra is not working properly, working on the art of public speaking will help you in balancing your throat chakra.

- Become more expressive

Start expressing your feelings. The more you keep your feelings to yourself, the greater the burden you'll put on your throat chakra. Don't keep suppressing your emotions. Speak your heart out, and that would help in restoring the balance in the throat chakra.

- Sky gazing

Gazing the blue sky can also be very helpful in restoring the balance in the throat chakra. The light blue sky energizes your throat chakra and helps in faster healing.

- Blue

BLUE THINGS ARE HELPFUL IN HEALING THIS CHAKRA, AND YOU CAN EAT BLUE FRUITS, AS WELL AS KEEP BLUE THINGS AROUND YOU FOR FASTER HEALING OF THE CHAKRA.

Yoga Asanas

Some of the important yoga asanas for healing chakra imbalance are:

- Bridge pose
- Triangle pose
- Camel Pose
- Warrior pose
- Extended side angle
- Plow pose
- Shoulder stand

Meditation

Meditation while chanting the seed mantra of this chakra 'Ham' is very helpful. Even guided meditations with visualizations are also very helpful in healing the imbalance in this chakra.

The longer you meditate on this chakra, the better the results would be. Your prime focus should be on bringing clarity in your speech.

Crystals

Lapis lazuli, iolite, turquoise, blue kyanite, aquamarine, celestite, and sodalite are some of the important crystals for treating imbalance in this chakra.

Essential Oils
Rosemary, frankincense, lavender, hyssop, and German chamomile are some of the important essential oils that can be used for healing this chakra.

Third Eye Chakra Healing

Lifestyle Changes
- Don't limit yourself

Third eye chakra brings to you immense possibilities. It opens millions of doors in front of you to do the same thing. It helps you in looking at things differently. If you start limiting yourself and questioning every action, you might put undue pressure on this chakra. Start thinking more courageously. Don't think with a limited perspective. Think in broader and wider terms. Don't think just about yourself, think about the greater good too. Expanding your limits of thinking can help in addressing the issues in this chakra.

- Work on balancing your brain

Third eye chakra is closely related to your brain and your mental faculties. However, when the third eye chakra is active, it would need a lot of activity to channelize the energy. It is important that you engage yourself in brain balancing activities to sharpen your brain.

- Work on your root chakra

Keeping your root chakra strong is very important for bringing a balance in your third eye chakra. This chakra can thin the line between reality and imagination. You can start imagining impossible things. You may not remain grounded and may start making impossible plans. You may also face problems in dealing with energies around you if your root chakra is not strong. If you want to keep your third eye chakra balanced, you should also work on keeping your root chakra stable and functioning.

- Don't rely on daydreaming

Third eye chakra can make you delusional at times. People start living in an imaginary world, and all that happens when they are not ready to handle the energies of this magnitude. Your mind and body should be prepared to deal with the energies of this intensity. You should stop daydreaming and start living in the real world.

- Be careful of negative influences

Third eye chakra increases your field of perception. This means that you start feeling the presence of other forms of energies around you. You start interacting with them more frequently. If your energy field is not very strong or if your root chakra is weak, you may get influenced by those energies. It is important that when your third eye chakra is out of balance, you remain careful of the kind of people and energies you interact with. You should immediately start work on strengthening your energy field.

- *Indigo*

INDIGO IS THE COLOR OF THIS CHAKRA, AND IT WOULD BE HELPFUL IF YOU COULD KEEP THINGS OF THIS COLOR AROUND YOU. IT WILL HELP IN STRENGTHENING YOUR ENERGY FIELD.

Yoga Asanas

There is no specific yoga that is more helpful in enhancing this chakra. You should focus on raising your consciousness level as much as possible. This chakra is more associated with intellectual and spiritual realization and less about physical manifestations. Try to build a greater focus.

Meditation

You can do specific third eye chakra meditations for better balancing of this chakra. You must work on reducing the influence of negative energies around you when you sit for meditation as your energy field can get weak at times. You must not fear anything while you mediate even if negative thoughts come to your mind.

Crystals

Lepidolite, sugilite, lapis lazuli, amethyst, fluorite, tanzanite, clear quartz, star sapphire, and kyanite can be helpful in balancing and healing this chakra.

Essential Oils

Frankincense, lavender, and sandalwood are effective in balancing this chakra.

Crown Chakra Healing

Lifestyle Changes

- Give respect to your elders

This is the topmost chakra that is associated with spiritual consciousness. If this chakra keeps functioning in a balanced manner, you will be highly respected, would have a healing touch, and possess great wisdom. You would always remain in a state of utmost pleasantness. It is like being blissful round the clock irrespective of the situation around you. However, if this chakra malfunctions, it can frustrate you. The best way to keep this chakra balanced is to respect others, especially your elders. When you show respect to your elders, it fills you with humility. That negates the buildup of negative energy.

- Be thankful

Remain thankful for everything in life. Don't be grumpy or sad. The more pleasantness you maintain, the more balanced the energies in this chakra would be.

- Do more charity

THE MORE YOU GIVE TO OTHERS, THE MORE YOU RECEIVE IN LOVE AND RESPECT. WHATEVER YOU GIVE AWAY IS THE REAL WEALTH YOU CAN EARN IN TERMS OF SPIRITUAL CONSCIOUSNESS. THEREFORE, IT IS IMPORTANT TO REMAIN INVOLVED IN CHARITABLE ACTIVITIES.

There are very few physical ways and tools to balance or heal this chakra. This chakra is almost outside your body and isn't controlled by physical things. The best way to keep this chakra balanced is to practice yoga and meditation. Both these activities can help a lot in keeping this chakra healthy and balanced.

Chapter 7 Reiki Healing
Healing through Hands

One of the benefits of learning to do Reiki is that you do not have to touch a person's body if it is not appropriate or if the person who is receiving Reiki is not comfortable with it. Your hands can be a couple of inches to a few feet away from the person's body. It depends on the situation and the individual's needs. A lot of times, it is more beneficial for the individual to receive Reiki off the body because they are supported. Their whole energy field is in a bubble of this healing energy.

An individual might also be in pain or just had surgery and is still recovering or is in a cast. In these situations, hands-on just does not feel comfortable, and hands-off is quite appropriate. Reiki goes through chairs and clothes, so there is no need for an individual to be sitting or lying in a special situation. It is very important that your patient gives you permission to do Reiki. You can't force Reiki. So whether you ask out loud or you ask in your mind's eye, they should give themselves the permission to receive.

As a Reiki practitioner, we just gently rest our hands on the body or off the body; and as a practitioner, again, it is important to get out of the way to let the energy flow. As we hold the space for the energy to flow, we may sense different phenomena. The recipient might sense a different energy. We just hold the position for one to three minutes; that is generally the prescribed duration for each hand position.

When a practitioner moves about, either on the body or off the body, it should be done with respect to boundaries. Giving Reiki in a chair is probably one of the most common forms of treatment, but Reiki can also be given on a massage table while a person is resting.

There's no time limit for treatment. It can be five minutes, or it can be an hour. And what's wonderful is that as a practitioner, you walk away from a treatment feeling energized yourself because you yourself are a channel receiving the energy first before the recipient. So it is win-win for both of you. If an individual has a troubled area, like a headache, you can apply your hands directly to that position. But also remember that Reiki goes exactly where it is needed. And at the end, the individual needs to be grounded and their energy field smoothed out, and both practitioner and recipient come back to the center. Again, Reiki treatment should end with the smoothing of the field, and that is always done off the body.

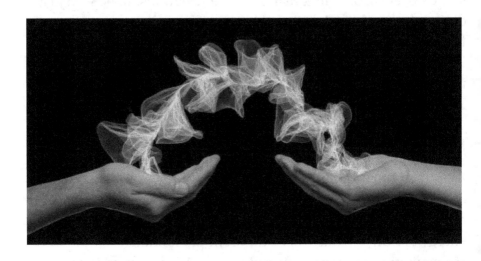

But still, if you are going to heal through hands, here is how you can do it:

Cup your hands around the top of the head while the patient is lying or sitting. Next, cup your hands around the ears. The next step is to surround the eyes of the patient with your hands. Next, cup the back of the head, and cup your hand around the throat. Leave a two-inch gap around the throat and place the hands above the heart chakra. Put your hands one in front of the other, and then place them on the solar plexus. Now place your hands across the belly button, which is the sacral chakra. For women, place a hand over each hip joint for the root chakra. For men, place a hand on either side of the hips to treat the root chakra. Next, place one hand on each knee and ask the client to turn over. Then place one hand in front of the other. Put the hands across the sacrum to treat the root chakra from the back. You can also treat the sacral chakra from the back. Also, it is possible to treat the solar plexus chakra from the back, as well as the heart chakra. Place the palms of your hands onto the soles of the feet. Finally, finish the Reiki treatment by brushing down the aura three times.

Reiki and color healing are also effective in treating other people. Reiki is light vibration. Color is light vibration. So together, the two amplify the amount of light healing that the individual is receiving. As a color treatment occurs, an individual may release various kinds of emotion from tears to laughter. Their own individual bodies may shake and release, so it is the responsibility of the practitioner to bring various colors in to coordinate the rainbow of the healing effect. So for example, the practitioner can bring in the color blue for a soothing and relaxing effect and red to amplify what is occurring. Violet or pink brings soothing, healing, and loving energy to balance out the session. When combined, color and Reiki create a tranquil, visual, wonderful atmosphere for relaxation to occur.

Another combination to heal others is Reiki and sound healing. Sound is vibration, and vibration combines with Reiki because Reiki is light vibration. Together, the two create a treatment session that can transport clients to another space where true cellular level healing can occur. Sound healing can take the form of background music during the session, or it can take the form of an individual reciting a chant or a mantra to that particular client. Sound healing can also work. You can do drumming, rattling, or didgeridoo. Percussive instruments tend to shift energy. They would be balanced by harmonious instruments, such as bowls, bells, or gongs that tend to smooth and reinforce an individual's energy field. Reiki and sound healing are new ways of working with both light and sound for an exponentially transcendent Reiki session.

Distant Healing

One of the most prominent things about Reiki is that it works on your aura or on your energy. Our body has various fields of energy vibrating at various lengths. And these energy fields often comprise of our emotions, thoughts, health, and spirituality. This energy can be sensed through hands as well, but this can be made possible through Reiki. Till now, you must know that our aura represents our state of overall health. So if a person is sick, he can be treated through Reiki. This method is usually called "distance Reiki healing."

How to Heal Someone through Distance Healing

Firstly, you need to empower your own body by Usui power symbol. Perform Reiki on your hands and chakra for a good ten to fifteen minutes. Remember the distance healing symbol from previous chapters? The next step is to visualize the distance healing symbol. After that, visualize the person on whom you want to do Reiki. Your intention must be to do Reiki on each level of that person for ten to twenty minutes.

In order to do Reiki to the person's physical level, imagine as if the Reiki energy enters in the crown chakra. The energy will enter the body slowly through the crown chakra. All the body parts will also be filled by the energy of Reiki. Imagine as if the person is glowing with that healing energy of Reiki.

After treating the person at a physical level, the next job is to treat him or her at the emotional level. At this part of distance healing, imagine as if that person is emotionally filled with joy, love, and contentment. Imagine that his or her glow is extended at the emotional level of his or her aura.

The next part is mental healing. You have to intend that his or her thoughts are calm and composed. He or she must have a clear mind. Imagine that the person's brain is working so profoundly and that thoughts are flowing quite easily. Imagine that he or she is able to find solutions to his or her problems. After that, imagine that person's worries leaving his or her body. Imagine Reiki energy filling up inside his or her body and treating his or her mental state of being.

The next level of distance healing is the spiritual level. Imagine as if Reiki energy is treating the person's soul. Imagine that he or she has a golden glow, both inside and out of the body. Imagine that the Reiki energy guides the person to get connected to his or her higher self. Imagine that the person's soul is reignited and is connected to the divine powers.

The entire process can also be performed by asking questions to the person before you send distance Reiki. Ask the person how he or she feels. Ask where the pain is, what his or her thoughts are. Ask whether he or she feels alone.

Chapter 8 Chakras Yoga

Yoga is one of the ways in which we can energize our chakras as well as align and balance them. By practicing yoga, we are also helping our spiritual, physical, and emotional attributes correspond to the chakra or frequency to get energized. Since chakras are also known to us as the 'spinning wheel,' it makes sense when we practice yoga because we release physical and emotional tension, which helps release the energy movement to flow freely. We will discuss specific yoga practices for each chakra:

Yoga for Root Chakra

Crow Pose

1. Stand and make sure your legs are three feet apart. Focus on your spine and feel it rising tall from the location of your pelvis. You will also feel the equal distribution of your weight between your feet on the surface of the ground or earth below you.

2. Squat slowly while maintaining the position of your feet on the earth. To help you maintain a straight posture, attach your palms together like a prayer posture, and place your elbows inside your two knees.

3. Inhale deeply and slowly into your abdomen, hold your breath for several minutes, and completely clear your lungs every time you exhale. Repeat this process for 20 to 30 minutes.

4. Release your hands, lie down and for a few minutes. Release the breath and let it continue to flow naturally. You will notice and feel prana moving through perineum physical area and other surrounding parts of your body, especially the coccyx and hips.

5. With more practice, you will master this root chakra yoga, and it will help you feel happy and worthy of your existence.

Yoga for Sacral Chakra

Pelvic Lifts

1. Lie down on the ground and ensure your spine is flat. Your head should also be on the ground as you face upwards. Feel your breath as it passes through your nostrils to your lungs, notice the movement of your rib cage as it goes up and down as you fill your lungs.

2. Bend the knees and let them point straight up in the sky. Ensure your souls that completely flat and close to your stretched arms on the ground. The palms of your hands should also touch the ground. You can also let your long middle finger touch your ankles to stay in the appropriate position.

3. Breathe in slowly and raise the pelvis to the highest level possible. Lift your spine gradually beginning with the lowermost vertebrae. Then slowly move the spinal column.

4. Exhale as you slowly move your spine downwards again to its original position.

5. Repeat this process of lifting your pelvis up and down for at least 20 minutes. Ensure the movement is steady, smooth, slow, and meditative. Your breath should lead the movement, ensure your lungs are filled, your spine and arms fully stretched and you are fully exhaling as you move back down. Allow your spine to be responsible for moving the rest of the body. Also, visualize all your tension been erased by your breath. Do at least 3 to 6 lifts.

6. Trust that all the movements you are feeling are meant to heal and bring balance and harmony. You will notice some changes and your sacral chakra will be successfully healed if your practice this form of yoga.

Yoga for Solar Plexus

Front Platform

1. Lie facing down with your stomach on the ground and toes pointing in the opposite direction or away from your head. Attach your palms to the ground as you bend your elbows.

2. Inhale and lift the body upwards as though you are doing a press up but with your toes still facing the opposite or backward direction.

3. Hold and stay in that upward position, start taking a deep breath and draw it into your abdomen and take

long exhales as you push your breath out. Practice this process for at least 3 minutes is focusing on and feeling the prana flowing through the navel center.

This yoga practice will help you in healing and balancing your solar plexus.

Yoga For Heart Chakra

Heart-Centering Meditation

1. Kneel and sit on your heels. Keep your spine in a straight position. Feel the flow of your breath as it fills your lungs as the diaphragm and solar plexus are lifted slightly.

2. Attach your middle fingers together as you extend your elbows sideways like flying wings and ensure your forearms stay parallel to the ground.

3. Lower your eyelids or close your eyes halfway and focus to gaze on your nose tip. The eye position is also widely used in other forms of yoga to focus, clear and silence the mind as well as activate pineal and pituitary glands.

4. You will hear vibrating inner voice in your mind with the mantra "Humme Hum Bram hum." You can also listen to the recorded version of this mantra while performing this type of yoga.

5. Extend your hands out slowly as you listen to this mantra. Inhale and exhale slowly and feel as the prana flows through the center of your heart and radiating to your entire body.

Yoga for Throat Chakra

Camel

1. Kneel on the floor and ensure your legs are apart. Gently place your palms on your ankles as you lean backward while maintaining the same position.

2. Breath in and allow your heart to be lifted upwards as your thighs and hips press forward.

3. During exhaling, draw your shoulders towards each other so that your heart opens more deeply. Place your hands on your back to make the exhaling process much easier.

4. Focus on your throat while breathing deeply and continue moving the hips forward to allow the sternum to open up.

5. Drop your head backward to its original position and comfortably return your hands in the ankle.

6. Relax and allow prana to heal your throat as it produces silent inward vibrating sound "hmmmmmmmmm" every time you exhale. Release the sound out and continue this process for at least three minutes or more.

7. Successful performance of this chakra will allow you to make conscious choices and communicate authentic expressions that come from our true sense.

Yoga for Third Eye Chakra

Guru Pranam

1. To start this yoga pose, sit on your heels, and sit in an upright position. Inhale and feel prana arriving with

every breath you take. You can use a firm pillow or blankets if you have difficulty sitting on your heels.

2. Extend your arms towards the ground as you comfortably spread your knees. Maintain the elongation of your spine by placing your forehead on the ground ahead and moving your lower back.

3. Focus on the vertebrae that are between the shoulders to enable the opening of the heart by melting that area.

4. Attach your palms together and visualize light as you inhale and exhale fully. Also, relax and let the force of gravity take control as well. Practice this yoga for at least 5 minutes or more.

5. Place your arms on the ground and gently lift your torso starting with the lowermost spine and rise up vertebra by vertebra and finish by lifting your head up. Before standing up, take a rest for a few minutes or lie on your back.

6. After practicing this type of yoga, you will feel the change and discover that you can easily use logic and make excellent decisions.

Yoga for Crown Chakra

Guru Prasad

1. Sit on your heels and feel your spinal column been filled with light and rise up the column. Take time to breathe in and feel as the prana flows through your breath.

2. Using your hands, make a bowl-shaped structure, and place your palms in front of your heart and face them

up towards the sky. The bowl's purpose is to receive invisible light.

3. Place your upper arms against your rib cage. Feel the gifts from the universe been poured into your hands. The gifts will come one after the blessings come to you in a similar manner. Feel the presence of the infinite universe as you practice this yoga.

4. Focus on your nose tip and lower eyelid to leave just a small opening in your eyes. The focus will help you to open your third eye, and your optic nerve is also stimulated with the pineal gland. However, as you continue with your meditation, you are free to close the eyes to enable you to focus more on your third eye.

5. Take long, deep breaths and exhale completely while allowing your heart to open for the feeling of love and compassion to penetrate through it.

6. Also, open yourself so that you can receive blessings in the form of many aspects, including consciousness and infinite universe.

7. Practice this form of mediation for at least 3 minutes. You can take more time if you feel you need it to heal your crown chakra completely.

8. Our consciousness will blossom if we allow the free flow of prana and healing of our crown chakra.

Malasana Yoga Pose

Squat and attach your palms together, breathe in deeply, hold for 30 seconds, and then exhale smoothly. Tuck the toes of your both feet and rest your chest on your knees as you practice this yoga pose. Don't lift your toes to get them out of the ground because it will disrupt your connection with the earth. This pose will help bring your being close to the earth, and the energy of the earth is felt through the feet while performing this practice.

Uttanasana

Stand up, fold your arms together by touching your right elbow with your left palm and doing the same with the left palm and touch your left elbow. Rest your folded hands on your head crown and then lean and bend forward at your waist with your folded arms and hands still intact. Ease your mind while practicing this yoga. This will enable us to find calmness and our center. It also releases tension from our entire back.

Mountain Pose

It is a chakra yoga practice that only involves standing up like a tree and feeling the support of the earth. This pose allows you to focus on the present moment and help us feel centered. Also, practice this yoga on the ground or grass to help you connect better and more with the earth.

Sun Salutations

It also resembles the pose of a cobra serpent. Lie down with your stomach on the ground. Using your palm hands, lift your upper part of your body (from the waist upwards while still lying down) face up to the sun. Inhale and exhale slowly, and you will start feeling connected, feel more sense of power and heat building up from within your body. You can choose to either close or open your eyes.

Anjaneyasana

This pose involves stretching your quad and psoas muscles. Its connection with the chakras makes sense because it's associated with the fight-or-flight mechanism. It is also connected with the first or the root chakra. Inhale and exhale five breaths to allow more time for your muscles to transmute residual flight or fight energy into a calm yet courageous inner strength.

Warrior II

Just like the name, pose like a warrior with your hands stretched outside and one leg stretched and the other slightly bent. The pose helps you dig deeper into your determination and strength.

Bridge Pose

Lie flat on the ground and lift your body using your upper back and support your pose with the souls of the feet firmly against the ground. This pose will help stimulate your throat chakra and help your root chakra to release excess energy. You can also use this pose while trying to balance your sacral, solar plexus, and the heart chakras.

Wide-Legged Forward Fold

Stretch your legs and lower your head to touch the ground while also supporting yourself with your hands. This pose will open your lower back and groin muscles. This will give an opportunity to your root chakra to release energy into your body.

Savasana

Lie down while facing upwards to allow total support by the earth beneath your body. Inhale and exhale smoothly while repeating the words 'I am safe, I am supported' with every cycle of your breathing. When we approach life from a grounded perspective, we tend to be more calm and happy, and this pose provides an opportunity to do just that while making us stronger within ourselves.

Chapter 9 Healing The Chakra With Colors

Colors have a lot to do with chakra healing, the brightness and dullness of a color have a certain effect on our mood, with certain colors associated with warmth and energy while other colors associated with coolness and calm, and everyone has their own preference in color. But how can colors have such a strong effect on chakra healing?

Every color has its own wavelength and frequency and has a different effect on people. This chapter will be devoted to the colors and the different ways you can make use of color to heal, uplift and energize your chakras.

The Colors

Red – Root Chakra
Red is the color for the root chakra and is widely viewed as the symbolic color for bravery, love and life. This color stimulates energy, brings warmth and helps you get connected to the root chakra.

Orange – Sacral Chakra
Orange, the next color up the spectrum, is a lighter version of red. It stimulates balance and sustains warmth. It can enhance sexuality, creativity and make you more sociable. It can even bring about happiness and make you more receptive to pleasures.

Yellow – Solar Plexus Chakra
The color associated with the sun, yellow, brings light energy into the body. It energizes and brightens the aura and it can help when you are engaged in grueling physical activity. Working on this energy chakra and color enhances well-being and creativity.

Green – Heart Chakra
The color green is associated with the heart chakra and is a color that can soothe the mind, body and spirit. To the mind, green

can be the most relaxing color. Green enhances the connection between man and the earth and of new life. A combination of cool and calming blue with the energy and life of yellow, green is the most balanced of all the colors. Visualizing breath in the color green maximizes healing and meditation. Visualizing this color associated with the heart chakra enhances focus, builds up compassion and empowerment, balances the energy and uplifts the mood.

Blue – Throat Chakra
Blue is a color that calms and relaxes both body and mind. It generates expansive energy that helps with relaxation. Blue is associated with thoughtful and deep love that is spiritual in origin. A good color for healing, especially in children, it is a good color for the home if you want to enhance calmness and quietness in the mind. Envisioning this color can help in the peaceful and truthful expression whether it is with words or in song.

Indigo – Brow Chakra
Often considered the color of royalty, indigo is associated with spiritual and higher consciousness. It has a deeply calming, almost tranquilizing effect, but it can cause depression if there is too much. This color, when associated with the brow chakra, can develop self-esteem, discernment, wisdom, develop intuition and give you clarity.

Purple Chakra – Crown Chakra
Considered to be the color of transformation, violet is a calming color that can help control nervousness and promote relaxation. You can also use this color to build up self-esteem. Working on the crown chakra with the color purple can stimulate dreams, bring clarity and connect you to your higher consciousness and spirituality.

Harness the Power of Colors

There are many ways to harness the power of colors and let them affect and change your energy levels, clear your chakras, balance your energy and change your mood. You will need this knowledge for you to know what chakras to work on during your therapy.

Chakra Balancing Color Therapy

Step 1: As per the usual, find a place where you can relax and not be disturbed for fifteen to thirty minutes. It has to be somewhere you are comfortable in and won't feel insecure or on your guard.

Step 2: Have seven pieces of cloth that correspond to each of your main energy chakras ready. Lie on your bed or the floor. Make sure that you can hold this position for 15 – 20 minutes without getting hot or cold.

Step 3: Relax. Close your eyes and take several slow deep breaths. With every breath, feel your body relax further.

Step 4: As you begin to feel your body relaxing, reflect back on your day in reverse, starting with when you laid down for your chakra color therapy, to when you woke up this morning.

Step 5: As you reflect on every moment of your day, think of the emotions you felt and the part of the body that felt affected. Identify what emotion it was you were dealing with and if you felt any physical pain that you associate with this type of emotion.

Step 6: Try to identify which chakra vortex was affected by this or that particular emotion. If needed, you can use a table or a list of emotions that particular chakras are responsible for.

Step 7: Once you have completely evaluated yourself and your chakras, it is time to start the color therapy. Open your eyes slowly and take the cloth that corresponds to the chakra center that you believe need energizing and place this over the corresponding main chakra center.

Step 8: Now, with the colored pieces of cloth over your main chakra points, it is time to visualize. Close your eyes and breathe deeply. As you take long slow breaths, feel the color from the pieces of cloth being absorbed by your chakra and drawn into the body. Start from the highest point. For example, if you feel deficiencies in your throat, navel, and root chakra, start with your throat, then go down until you reach the lowest point.

Step 9: As you visualize this, feel your energy centers balance out and become re-energized. Feel the corresponding organs and organ systems become active and vital, feel your chakras balance out.

Step 10: Continue this visualization technique for 5 - 10 minutes or until you feel balanced as a whole and feel your ailments dissipate. Repeat these steps as needed (whenever you feel an imbalance in your body or if you feel a little emotional etc.).

Full Color Chakra Strengthening Therapy

Now that you've taken care of any imbalances with your chakra, you can move on to a full color chakra therapy that will strengthen and revitalize your whole chakra system using cloth swatches that correspond with your energy chakras.

Step 1: Again, find a comfortable place where you can sit quietly for 10 - 15 minutes. It has to be a place you are familiar and comfortable in.

Step 2: Take all the pieces of cloth and place each one over the part of your body here its corresponding chakra center can be found.

Step 3: Take slow, deep breaths and visualize your chakra centers vibrantly glowing with its corresponding color. Imagine your body bathed in rainbow light.

Step 4: While you visualize yourself bathed in rainbow, feel your body strengthened, and feel your chakras becoming re-energized. Feel how all your chakras are becoming balanced and in harmony with each other. Feel how your physical body is deeply connected with your spiritual mind. Feel your illnesses and discomforts fade away as you absorb the colors of the cloth. Focus your awareness on the glowing energy building up inside you, as well as how your body is becoming balanced.

Step 5: Continue in this state of visual color therapy for ten minutes, or until you feel completely balanced, energized and strengthened. Repeat this therapy when you feel the need, although it would be a good idea to fix any imbalance first with chakra balancing color therapy first before you do the full body full color therapy.

Other things you can do with Color:

There are other ways to influence your chakra with color without having to meditate on it.

Wear clothes in the color that correspond to that chakra
If it happens that you want to strengthen your root chakra, you can wear red. If you want to become calm, you can wear blue. Refer to the notes above regarding chakras and emotions associated with a certain color.

Use the colors in your environment
You can decorate your room or your office with certain colors that correspond to a chakra center that you feel you have to strengthen. You can use flowers or plants.

Color the light

You can use colored light bulbs or stained glass to give you access to the color that you want to infuse into your body. You can even try to do the chakra strengthening yoga position while bathed in the color of the chakra you want to balance. Do this with caution though and make sure to balance your chakras rather than overly favor one in particular.

Using colors to heal and strengthen your chakras is a fun and easy way to find balance in your energies. Incorporating color therapy with your kundalini yoga poses can bring you health and energy, as well as slowly and safely awaken the kundalini energy within you.

Chapter 10 Healing The Chakra With Sounds

Sounds can heal and balance your chakras, too. Just like colors, sounds have distinct wavelengths and frequencies to which the seven energy centers respond to. The therapeutic sounds include the ones you create and the sounds from your surroundings. Think of songs, chants, prayers, music and the sounds present in natural landscapes such as oceans, forests and meadows.

Sound healing or therapy has been employed in Western, Oriental and African cultures since the ancient times. These days, healing sounds and music are used primarily for relaxation, whether you have a medical condition or are simply under stress. However, the belief that sounds have chakra healing and balancing properties comes from early Chinese, Tibetan and Indian medicines.

There are different ways to heal and balance your chakras with the help of sounds. The most notable ones are: chakra toning and bija mantras. There are also various tools whose sounds can benefit the energy centers in your body.

Chakra Toning

Chakra toning is a technique that makes use of vowel sounds to clear and balance the energy centers. You can do this every day to be more familiar with the natural harmonics from the vowels. In speech, there is a thing called information energy. The vowels work as the carriers of information energy while the consonants are the breakers of the energy flow. In ancient Chinese, Hebrew and Sanskrit, vowels are also deemed as sacred because they bear the focus and intention in speech.

Before you begin toning your chakras, you should find a place where no one can disturb you and where you cannot disturb anyone. You should also get rid of possible sources of noises such as gadgets, clocks and running appliances.

Step 1: To start, sit comfortably on the floor or ground. You may use a mat or cushion. Keep your back straight to facilitate uninterrupted energy flow from one chakra to another. It also helps to visualize your head floating above a cord and your body hanging below.

Step 2: Before you make the sounds, channel your focus, energy and intent to each chakra. Take a deep breath. Let your lower stomach expand as you inhale.

Step 3: Gently utter the sounds. It is up to you to decide the frequency. When you make the sounds, feel your body for resonance—except for the throat because it will always vibrate—to get the right pitch. The right pitch differs every now and then. It actually depends on a variety of factors such as diet, mood, personality and personal activities. Do it slowly and calmly. Do not strain your voice.

- For the root chakra, utter your deepest "UUH" sound akin to the vowel sound of "cup".

- For the sacral chakra, utter an "OOO" sound that is similar to the vowel sound of the word "you". In terms of pitch, this is slightly higher than the guttural sound for the first chakra.

- For the solar plexus chakra, utter an "OH" sound that is like the vowel sound for the word "go".

- For the heart chakra, utter an "AH" sound. The said sound deemed as an embodiment of passion which is an aspect of the heart chakra.

- For the throat chakra, utter an "EYE" sound that is similar to the vowel sound in "my". Do not make the mistake of associating the said sound to your third eye chakra.

- For the third eye chakra, utter an "AYE" sound that is like the vowel sound in "say".

- For the crown chakra, utter the highest "EEE" sound you can produce.

Interestingly, when you try to tone from the "UUH" to "EEH" sounds quickly and continuously, you will notice that it forms the word "why".

Step 4: Visualize the energy in each breath to come into your body and pass through your target chakra.

Step 5: Once you are done, sit still for at least 10 minutes for the energy to sink into your chakras. When you feel dizzy afterwards, probably due to the prolonged sitting, tone an extensive "aaaah" sound to direct the energy back to your heart chakra. Then tone using an extensive "ooooh" sound to drive it to your lower chakras.

Bija Mantra

A mantra is made up of one or more sounds, syllables or words. It is often uttered during meditation but you can resort to it anytime for that little push you need to go on with the rest of the day. The name mantra is a combination of two Sanskrit words namely man, which means to think, and tra, which means instruments or tools. Therefore, the literal translation of mantra could be an instrument or tool for thought. Aside from being an instrument for thought, mantra is deemed to have the ability to transform.

Historically, the singing bowls were made in Nepal and China, particularly in the Himalayan regions in the said countries. These days though, the said instruments are also manufactured in other countries such as Japan and Korea.

A Tibetan singing bowl comes with a ringer that you are going to use to create the sounds that your chakras will respond to. Each pack of singing bowl sold these days also contains a pamphlet where the information on how to get the right frequency and pitch is provided. Your chakra will vibrate to a certain tune from the singing bowl. To give you an overview, the higher tones are for the higher chakras while the lower tones are for the lower chakras.

You can buy this instrument from a specialty store. You may also get one online. Of the different Tibetan singing bowls out there, Remuna and Thadobati are the recommended types for chakra balancing. These singing bowls are among the smallest, thinnest and most lightweight types. Because of their size, thinness and weight, you can easily hold one Remuna or one Thadobati bowl and ring it.

You may also visit a practitioner of chakra healing using the said instruments. You will be asked to lie down. The practitioner will place a bowl at the top of or beside your chakra. He will ring it according to the most suitable frequency for each chakra.

Tibetan singing bowls are not made specifically for chakras. Therefore, you can use them for other sound therapies such as sound bathing.

Guided Meditation

The most obvious way of using sounds to heal and balance chakras is through guided meditation or visualization. As its name suggests, this requires a professional who is guiding you as you meditate to heal and balance your chakras. You can buy prerecorded guided meditations, pay for meditation classes, or take advantage of free options available online. Just make sure the guided meditations you are using are tailormade to clear and balance your chakras. If you are quite new to meditation practices in general, the guided meditation can familiarize you with the train of thoughts you should be having as you meditate.

Additional Ways to Meditate Using Sounds:

Aside from listening to guided meditation, you can also meditate to clear and balance your chakras with certain sounds in the background. These sounds may come from musical instruments which may be playing live or prerecorded. Shabd sounds are also beneficial to your chakras. These sounds are comprised of unstrucked melodies, meaning they are usually formed without human intervention. The right shabd sounds, keynotes and frequencies for each chakra are as follows:

Root Chakra

    Shabd Sounds: Earthquake or Thunder
    Keynote: C
    Frequency: 256 Hz.

Sacral Chakra

    Shabd Sound: Ocean
    Keynote: D
    Frequency: 288 Hz.

Solar Plexus Chakra

    Shabd Sound: Roaring Fire
    Keynote: E
    Frequency: 320 Hz.

Heart Chakra

    Shabd Sound: Wind
    Keynote: F
    Frequency: 341.3 Hz.

Throat Chakra

Shabd Sound: Crickets

Keynote: G

Frequency: 384 Hz.

Third Eye Chakra

Shabd Sounds: Space or Bells
Keynote: A
Frequency: 426.7 Hz.

Crown Chakra

Shabd Sound: Om
Keynote: B
Frequency: 480 Hz.
Using sounds to balance your chakras is quite challenging. In some instances, having the wrong vibrations can supply your chakras with excess energies. The imbalance causes offsets the positive effects that the sounds are supposed to give. You should always observe caution when you resort to sound therapies to heal, clear and balance your energy centers. Nonetheless, there are harmless ways to use sounds for your chakra meditation. One of those ways is listening to the sounds of waves heating the shores.

Chapter 11 Crystal Healing

Balancing your chakras can be done in many ways, and typically you will want to use several methods in order to restore and maintain balance within' your chakras. A very common way to bring balance to your chakras is with crystals. You can use crystals in many ways, and they have the wonderful advantage of not requiring you to do too much to gain the benefits from them. You can keep them nearby, in your pocket, or wear them as jewelry to gain the benefits from these healing stones. You may also specifically work with them such as through meditation or affirmations to assist you in bringing balance to your chakras.

Crystals You Can Use

Each chakra has its own set of crystals associated with it. The following lists show you the most common crystals associated with each chakra. Please note these lists are not exhaustive. You will find more in-depth information below about using other crystals, and picking which crystals to use.

Root Chakra Stones

- Hematite
- Garnet
- Black Tourmaline
- Zircon
- Black Obsidian
- Smoky Quartz
- Jet
- Red Jasper

Sacral Chakra Stones

- Carnelian
- Blue-Green Turquoise
- Copper
- Blue-Green Fluorite
- Imperial Topaz
- Orange Calcite
- Vanadinite

Solar Plexus Chakra

- Citrine
- Yellow Jasper
- Amber
- Gold Tiger's Eye
- Golden Calcite
- Yellow Appatite

Heart Chakra

- Rose Quartz
- Pink Danburite
- Vesuvianite
- Lepidolite

- Watermelon Tourmaline
- Jade
- Malachite
- Rosasite
- Pink/Rubellite Tourmaline
- Green Aventurine
- Cobaltian Calcite

Throat Chakra

- Blue Calcite
- Sodalite
- Angelite
- Blue Chalcedony
- Blue Lace Agate
- Aquamarine
- Amazonite
- Blue Turquoise
- Chrysocolla
- Celestite
- Blue Kyanite

Third Eye Chakra

- Tanzanite
- Azurite
- Lapis Lazuli

Crown Chakra

- Quartz
- Herkimer Diamond

- Selenite
- White Howlite
- White Hemimorphite
- White Danburite
- White Topaz
- White Calcite
- Amethyst
- Apophyllite

Picking Crystals

There are many more crystals beyond what was listed above, and you may wish to use any number of them. Alternatively, you may struggle to decide exactly which one to use since there are so many to choose from. There are many ways to pick your crystals, to be exact. However, there are a few things you should consider to help you pick exactly which one can benefit you for the specific purpose that you are searching for.

First, you should understand that your intuition will often draw you to exactly what you need in your life. This is true in two ways: one, you will want to choose the one you are most drawn to. It is likely that you need this in your life. Two, you should also consider the stone you are most drawn away from. These often carry an additional important piece of information that you need to consider, as well.

Next, if you are choosing stones that are not on the list but you want one for a specific chakra, look for stones that correlate with the colors of the chakras. Remember, though, the root chakra can be associated with red, black or brown. The throat chakra is typically associated with lighter blues and the third eye chakra is the darker blues. The crown chakra can be associated with purple or white. When you choose a stone, you can choose based off of the color to pick one for each chakra, or for the specific chakra you want to consider.

Another way you can pick your stone is based on its unique healing abilities. Although each stone falls under a specific chakra, they do have their own independent abilities. For example, the amethyst stone is amazing for protection and the quartz stone is wonderful for clarification. Still, both are used for the crown chakra. The same rings true for virtually every stone, so if you have a specific ailment you may wish to find a stone that will work specifically with that ailment.

How to Use Crystals

Using crystals is easy, and there are many ways that you can do so. Crystals are one of the most versatile healing formats for the energy body and can be used with intention and then in almost any way to assist in healing. The following are some of the most common ways to use them.

Meditate with Them

One way that you can really gain a lot of benefit from crystals is to meditate with them. You can hold them in your hand or simply keep them nearby. Often when you are meditating with crystals you will want to keep your gaze on them, as opposed to closing your eyes. However, you can still close your eyes if you desire. If you want to work with all of your chakras, you may consider lying on your back and placing a stone over each chakra and then lying that way for a while until you feel as though your chakras have been aligned and balanced once again.

Keep Them Nearby

Crystals have powerful energies and you can gain the energies simply by having them around. You can keep a piece of a crystal nearby, keep a small bowl of them, or otherwise keep them in your presence. You may want to place crystals in certain places to bring certain energies to those places. For example, you may wish to put black obsidian by the door to keep negative energies out of your house, and rose quartz by your bed to keep you peaceful and calm when you are sleeping. There are many different crystals that you can keep nearby, depending on what you are trying to achieve. Some prefer to put them out them put them away when they are done, whereas others prefer to keep them out permanently.

Wear Them

A very common and powerful way to use crystals is to have them resting against your skin. You can do this by wearing them as jewelry. You can wear earrings, necklaces, bracelets, rings or any other form of jewelry with these crystals within' them and wear them. Some people wear them only with a specific purpose and others wear them on a daily basis. It is said that when crystals are directly against your skin, you absorb the maximum benefit from them.

Keep Them in Your Pocket

If you are not one to wear jewelry, you may wish to keep the stones in your pocket or in a medicine bag instead. This way, you can keep them nearby and still have them to use. Some people even like to carry around worry stones, which are crystals that you keep in your pocket and when you need a stronger "dose" of their energy, you can simply rub your thumb or fingers through the indentation in the stone.

There are many reasons and uses for crystals, just as there are many ways you can use them. Some people even allow them to "steep" in water and then drink the water to gain their benefits. Of course, you would want to make sure the crystal was clean before doing this. However, it goes to show that there are virtually limitless ways to gain the positive energies from these stones and gain the value that they have to offer. Crystals are one of the most powerful and useful natural healing "remedies" available, and pretty much everyone can benefit from their many uses. Whether you want a gentle rebalancing or if you want to completely heal an unaligned chakra, crystals can offer you a world of help.

Spiritual Affirmations

The power of prayer and the power of spoken word are extremely powerful. You can use spoken words or affirmations to assist you in creating a balance within' your chakras and setting intentions for what you wish to achieve. You can use these affirmations either mentally or verbally and gain value from them, as the primary point is to release the intention for them into your life. Affirmations have been scientifically proven to assist in clearing and focusing the mind which can bring about a great deal of value when you are looking to heal your life.

What is an Affirmation?

Affirmations are short sayings or mantras that you can use on a regular basis to create a specific focus and intention in your life. Generally, you want to say an affirmation out loud and at least three times to gain benefit from it. The more you say it, the better they work. Additionally, you want to use a great deal of intention and emotion behind your affirmations. While you could simply say it, it is best if you say it with purpose and meaning. The more you believe in the affirmation, the more power it will have when it comes to balancing and healing your chakras and your life.

Which Affirmation Should I Use?

Each chakra has its own governing bodies, emotions, and symptoms; therefore, each chakra also has its own type of affirmations you would want to use with it. The following are affirmations that you can use specifically with each chakra.

The Root Chakra

"I am balanced in life"

"I am safe and secure"

"I am firmly grounded"

"I trust"

"I am responsible for my own body"

The Sacral Chakra

"I create freely"

"I have healthy feelings"

"I lovingly appreciate and accept myself as I am"

"I am loveable"

"I am strong"

The Solar Plexus Chakra

"I am enough"

"I take pride in my accomplishments and for who I am"

"I am confident"

"I am powerful"

"I honor and respect myself and my choices"

The Heart Chakra

"I love myself and the world around me"

"I open myself up to receive love, infinitely"

"I give love freely"

"My heart is full of love"

"I heal my heart and life with love"

The Throat Chakra

"I speak my truth effortlessly"

"I am honest with my words"

"I speak lovingly and kindly"

"I claim my own voice"

"My story is my own"

The Third Eye Chakra

"I am an intuitive being"

"I trust my intuition and inner guidance"

"I see the world clearly as it is"

"I see myself for who I truly am"

"I manifest all that I desire into my reality"

The Crown Chakra

"I am a divine being"

"I am connected to spirit"

"I am a limitless and infinite being"

"I am balanced"

"I am deeply connected to spirit and the universe"

Can I Use Other Affirmations?

The above affirmations are a wonderful idea of where to start, but you can certainly go ahead and create your own affirmations. In fact, creating your own affirmations is a wonderful way to increase the power behind your affirmations and therefore the effectiveness of them. The real power behind affirmations comes from believing in what you are saying. Therefore, when you create your own affirmations it becomes even easier to believe in what you are saying and gain value from them. Your affirmations can correlate to anything surrounding the chakra that you are intending to work with, or all of them if you intend to do so.

How Can I Increase the Effectiveness of Affirmations?

Of course, saying affirmations on its own is powerful. But, there are certainly ways to increase the amount of power behind saying them. For starters, having true meaning and purpose behind them is a good way. If you say an affirmation without meaning it, it may not work. Or, it may take longer to work because you must first develop the ability to believe in what you are saying. If you say it with conviction and belief from the get-go, you will increase the effectiveness.

Another way to increase the effectiveness of your affirmations is to say them out loud, especially in front of a mirror where you are looking at yourself. If you get into a power stance, you further increase the conviction behind them and therefore the power within' them. You can do so by putting your hands high in the air as if you were about to start cheering and then confidently say each affirmation to yourself. Then, you can physically see yourself commanding each affirmation and the confidence within' yourself. This further increases your ability to believe it, hold yourself accountable, and thus gain value from it.

Affirmations are a powerful speech method that enables you to change your life through spoken word. You can use affirmations for virtually anything, and you may even wish to use several at once. Ideally, you should use them on a regular basis, at least daily. The more you do, the more you will benefit from them.

Chapter 12 Personality Analysis Using Psychological Astrology

Crystal gazing can edify our conduct and explain relationships throughout everyday life. Nonetheless, it can't and shouldn't bind an individual. A celestial birth picture comprises of images that have been converted into words and solid models in the accompanying content.

When understanding them, you will find inconsistencies. For instance, one segment portrays the requirement for a quiet and stable relationship, and another area says that you need incitement and assortment inside a relationship. Such a logical inconsistency contains the requesting challenge to express the two alternate extremes. The accompanying content isn't a "fortune-telling horoscope" since only you are the modeler of your predetermination. The horoscope depicts the "crude material" that you have accessible.

Ascendant in Capricorn

With the ascendant in Capricorn, you establish a dependable and genuine connection. You seek security and acknowledge progressive systems. Individuals believe you to be somebody who pays attention to life, making progress toward objectives in a restrained and mindful way.

Sun in Libra

In your deepest being, you take a stab at equity, agreement, and harmony. Your prudent and approachable way gives you a chance to be prevalent with numerous individuals. Disposing of contentions is one of your worries. In doing as such, you can create extensive discretionary capacities in the event that you face the contention and don't just accommodate for harmony. You are great at moving toward other individuals. Simultaneously, you generally underscore what you share for all intents and purpose and what interfaces you with them. You frequently give too little consideration to the distinctions.

Sun in The Ninth House

You might want to genuinely apply the characteristics depicted above and along these lines extend your own frame of reference. Framing conclusions, issues concerning theory and training, and outside societies, just as the trade with individuals who think contrastingly and are critical to you, similar to the probability of persuading others regarding your feelings.

Moon in Leo

Your forces of the creative mind are very enthusiastic. You consider each to be a circumstance as a component of a more prominent setting and respond in like manner with emotional signals. With your regular warmth, you can be extremely winning. Since you esteem consideration, you will in general now and again place yourself a lot at the focal point of consideration.

Moon in The Seventh House

You have an incredible requirement for being as one and feel increasingly comprehensive when you are seeing someone. Your interceding way should make it simple for you to build up contacts. You endeavor to adjust and underline what you share practically speaking with others and what associates you with them. On the off chance that you react an excessive amount to other individuals, you will experience issues in inclination your own needs.

Mercury in Libra

You are a representative and don't care for transparently defying someone else in a discussion. With respect and natural seeing, for all intents and purposes in a hidden way, you endeavor to tell another person your supposition. At the point when you are engaged with a discussion with somebody, you stress what you share practically speaking; you want to dismiss contrasts.

Mercury in The Ninth House

You need to share your contemplations and learning. With your scholarly and verbal capacities, you might want to rouse and persuade others. Along these lines, you are presumably fit for functioning as an instructor, teacher, or sales representative.

Venus in Virgo

Excellence is intently connected with handy contemplations for you. Wonderful things that are just there to satisfy the eye effectively motivation you to address whether they merit spending the cash on them. Delightful things ought to likewise satisfy a reason. Then again, you have certain tasteful measures for the articles of day by day use, making both a down to earth and delightful condition for yourself.

Venus in The Eighth House

You don't have a lot of enthusiasm for a shallow relationship. You need to have energy and sexuality and furthermore live it out. At the point when you go into an association, you request an absolute commitment from your accomplice; one could nearly say that you need to have the person in question. You have a sharp eye for what is covered and covered up in an organization. You need to test your accomplice's dull sides. On the off chance that your accomplice has a past that you don't think about, you will scarcely disregard the person in question until you know it all.

Mars in Gemini

Most importantly, you stand up for yourself by utilizing words. Correspondence is a method for you to make things occur; it could nearly be known as a weapon for your situation. You rationally create fight plans and use them to intentionally advocate for yourself in discussions. You acknowledge vivacious dialogs and can likewise contend when you get irritated.

Mars in The Sixth House

With extraordinary likelihood, the sort of man who captivates you exemplifies huge numbers of these characteristics. This implies you like down to earth, reasonable, and reasonable men with whom you can ace regular day to day existence and achieve an occupation. An adoration relationship that additionally empowers you to fill in as a group ought to especially speak to you.

Jupiter in The Seventh House

You like having your accomplice bolster you since this makes it workable for you to show yourself as liberal and hopeful. You bring a significant inclination to venture into a relationship, which isn't constantly good with the social ideas of organization and marriage. You will, in general, take a gander at an organization from the light side and show little ability to chip away at common issues together.

Saturn in The Sixth House

Fundamentally, your assignment is to accept accountability for your reality, which means for your day-by-day life, your body, and your wellbeing. This doesn't imply that you must be impeccable. Maybe you can likewise force yourself to assign certain undertakings and along these lines decrease the weight and requests without anyone else execution.

Uranus in The Fifth House

You look for conceivable outcomes for articulation that don't relate to the standard. Do you like to play-act? You enjoy changing yourself. You appreciate more than once showing yourself in an alternate getup. You are inventive and have the inclination to show yourself off.

Neptune in The Eighth House

It is hard for you to effectively evaluate social qualities and power structures. On the off chance that you manage acquired cash or different qualities that have been endowed to you, you may effortlessly believe this to be a typical property. It might potentially go through your hands.

Pluto in The Seventh House

"Win big or bust!" is your witticism seeing someone. Your accomplice needs to have you totally - or you need that person totally - with body, brain, and soul. Your connections are serious and energetic. This likely additionally incorporates the dread of being left and the endeavor to control and control the relationship and the accomplice. An affection relationship without power games, without testing each other's quality, without energy, and without envy resembles a soup without salt for you.

Chapter 13 Questions That Arise on The Healing Path

Ascension is what you call the process of aligning with your true energy as a soul. Working towards ascension brings you into direct contact with how to heal your chakra energy and what must be done in order to align your energy with the light of your whole life purpose. As you begin to heal and balance your energy system, you will have to go through a long quest for information from yourself and through your inner emotions, feelings, thoughts, and experiences from your life up to this point.

The questions you need to ask are the kind of questions a therapist might ask you in a healing session. They are designed to guide you on the right path to helping yourself heal and clear all of the blocks from within you. If you think about it, working with a "talk" therapist in a counseling session is exactly like the work you do to heal your chakras through the lessons and meditations you have already learned about. You are your closest counselor and ally and have the power to begin answering your own questions about how you feel, what you think and what is lurking under the surface of your existence as a person in society.

In this chapter, you will answer the questions outlined for you as though a therapist is asking you how you are feeling about your life. The questions will be directly associated with each chakra to help you concentrate on the specific energy of each one. As you practice your clearing and balancing techniques, you can start to incorporate these questions into your meditations, connections, and considerations. Open your journal and answer the questions for the chakra you are currently working on. You don't have to do it in the order they are listed here.

Root Chakra

When do I feel the most at peace with myself?

When do I feel the security I need the most?

How long has it been since I have felt financially secure?

When was the last time I had a good cry?

How long has it been since I felt good about my life purpose or my path?

What happened in my early life or childhood that could have made me feel less secure?

How many minutes a day do I devote to myself alone?

When are my most joyful moments about my security and my financial situation?

How hard do I try to set aside time for the things I truly want and desire to have in my life?

How do I set myself up for a better home life that fits my basic needs?

Sacral Chakra

How long has it been since I let myself feel my whole body from head to toe?

When do I feel the best in my body and my sense of sexuality?

How often do I allow myself physical or emotional pleasure?

What sensations make me feel the most alive and free?

How long has it been since I have done anything creative?

When was the last time I danced or moved my body to music?

Are my feelings about my life something that I deny and ignore, or embrace and explore?

Are there any times when I feel afraid to be naked with myself and my body, or with other people?

When do I give myself the time to truly embrace, hold, and love myself?

How often do I let myself sense all of the things in my life by touching them? (ex: petting a cat, feeling the fabric of your sofa or living room furniture, carefully feeling the vegetables or fruits you are going to chop to eat for dinner, caressing your house plants, feeling water coming out of the faucet and enjoying the sensation).

Solar Plexus Chakra

Do I allow myself to show off my talents in front of others?

Am I only okay with subjects that make me look good in front of other people?

Do I have a history of alcohol/substance abuse or addiction?

Are there times in my life when I have felt weak around other confident people?

Am I allowed to give myself the time to openly act as my true self, even when I am afraid of other people's judgments?

Do I have the ability to stay focused on my goals and intentions?

How many self-help lessons have I taken to try and improve myself but have not succeeded in the way that I am hoping?

When I am my most honest with myself?

When do I feel the proudest of my life?

Am I able to let other people be as strong and powerful as I am?

Heart Chakra

When was the last time I truly felt loved by anyone?

Am I giving myself the love that I want, or am I asking it to come from other people more often?

Am I open to receiving love and friendship from other people, or do I have a hard time feeling open with other people?

Am I able to love someone unconditionally, or do I have strict parameters about how love should be?

When was the last time I said: "I love myself"?

How long has it been since I gave myself a loving embrace and gave myself a pat on the back for all of my hard work as a mother, father, friend, employee, partner, etc.?

Have all of my relationships ended in a negative way or left me feeling a lot of heartache and sorrow?

When was the last time I had a relationship with someone that had a positive feeling of love?

Where am I the most vulnerable in my relationships with others? (ex: jealousy, self-confidence, communication, sexuality, etc.)

How well do I know my own heart and the truth of what I actually want to have in love and relationships?

Throat Chakra

What are my least favorite words and why do I dislike them so much?

When was the last time I shouted out loud or screamed because I needed to release something?

How many times in my life have I wanted to say something but then decided not to?

What did I do in my childhood to express myself and was there a time that I was told not to by my parents, teachers, or friends?

When was my last attempt at singing for fun and pleasure?

How long has it been since I told myself, or someone else, a lie?

What kind of sentences do I use to describe my feelings? Are they long and elaborate, or short and uninformative?

When someone asks me about myself, am I able to easily talk about my life or do I quickly change the subject?

How often do I tell myself that what I am saying is stupid or dumb?

When is my favorite time to talk to someone? (ex: after a crisis, over a casual meal, right before bed, all of the time, etc.)

Brow Chakra

How many times have I felt myself thinking a thought and then telling myself that it is stupid or impossible?

How well do I know my real thoughts, attitudes, beliefs, and values?

Are my ideas a question of the reality that I live in, or do I just decide to follow what everyone else is thinking or doing?

When am I the most content with how I think and feel about my life?

Are my ideas good enough for me, or are they supposed to fit into what other people want and desire?

Do I believe in my psychic abilities, or do I think that these things are impossible?

Have I ever told myself a certain word or phrase over and over again to train myself to think a certain way? (ex: "I am not smart enough." "I am not good enough." "I don't have all the things I need to accomplish anything I want." "I am a failure.")

Have I ever seen objects, lights, visions, or other energies that are not usually perceived by other people, or with the naked eye?

When was the last time I had a dream I could remember?

What is the most intense dream or vision I have ever had and how did it affect me?

Crown Chakra

How long has it been since I felt a flower petal and enjoyed its beauty?

When was the last time I gazed at my own reflection and saw a beautiful light in my eyes?

How many years has it been since I had faith in something bigger than myself?

How long ago did I let go of my love for life and all of the people, places, animals and things in this world?

Have I ever allowed myself to be truly open to my own personal spirituality?

Have I allowed myself to be brainwashed by other people's ideals about religion or faith?

How long ago did I give myself permission to leave my whole light and live as something less than my true self?

What was my first major experience with spirituality?

How long ago did I feel like there was nothing in the universe and that we are all alone, or did I feel like we are not alone, but felt like there was no point in knowing it anyway?

When do I allow myself time to appreciate the beauty and magic of all life on the planet and in the universe?

Whole Body, Mind, Spirit
1. When do I fell the most aligned with my whole self?

2. Where do I hold the most tension in my being: physical body, emotions or feelings, thoughts, and ideas, or faith?
3. What lives have I lived before this current life that may have affected my whole energy system? (ex: past life karma, patterns of behavior from another soul life)
4. Where so I look for guidance for my whole being: inside of myself, or outside of myself?
5. What is the nature of my greatest wound and how does it affect my whole self?
6. How well do I know my true feelings from all of the experiences I have had in my life so far, and how do they relate to my current state of feeling and behaving?
7. When was the last time I gave myself a chance to ask for help from someone or something (spirit guides) else?
8. What is my purpose and am I already living it?
9. When I am alone, do I feel happy, sad, doubtful, fearful, or another emotion, or emotions?
10. How well do I trust the answers I have given to all these questions, from the root to the crown?

All of these questions are a great beginning to digging deeper into the true source of your energy blockages in your chakras. Healing yourself means communicating with yourself on all levels. It is not just about how you meditate or perform your rituals or visualizations; you must also talk to yourself, ask yourself important and probing questions, even when you fear the answer. The truth of you is always better than a lie, and so it becomes the object of healing your chakras to seek out the truth of who you truly are underneath it all.

Ask more questions about yourself and develop your own methods about how you connect and communicate with your energy. It is only the beginning of a lifelong bond with your whole chakra system and the energy of your life.

Chapter 14 Secret Tips for Third Eye Chakra

We've talked about the Third Eye in the context of the whole chakra system. But this chakra is quite different from the others around it. The five chakras below it are much more concerned with the material world, and how you interact and experience that. But the Third Eye is something else: the gateway to a whole new, spiritual world.

The Third Eye is perhaps the chakra most shrouded in mystery. Much of our knowledge about it has been passed down throughout history, with some of the knowledge dating back to ancient civilizations.

The Ancient Greek doctor and philosopher Galen wrote about the third eye back in ancient times. He reports that his colleagues say the pineal gland, the gland located next to the third eye, as regulating psychic energy. He only saw the gland as regulating blood flow, however.

In Hindu culture, the god Shiva and other deities are represented as having a literal third eye on their forehead. This is a symbol for enlightenment, the ability of these gods to see into the higher realms.

The Third Eye also crops up in Ancient Egyptian culture as the sacred Eye of Ra and Eye of Horus. This eye was drawn on the center of the forehead on sarcophagi, the coffins in which the mummies of the pharaohs were placed. This, similarly, was seen as the eye of the important gods Ra and Horus, symbolizing a connection to the divine.

The Third Eye is often symbolized as a pinecone, because of its eye-like shape and connection to sacred geometry. In this case we see a lot of pinecone imagery in ancient civilizations as well. Ancient Sumerian gods are often depicted with a pinecone, as is the ancient Greek god Dionysus, who is associated with expanded consciousness and moving beyond the material world.

Additionally, there is a recurring symbol in the ancient world of two serpents rising up to meet a pinecone. In Ancient Egypt, this was the staff of Osiris. This can be interpreted as the energy in the body rising up to meet the Third Eye and enlightenment.

Even today, in the Catholic Church, the pinecone carries great symbolic weight. You can see one atop the staff of the Pope.

The presence of pinecones and serpents together in such abundance has caused some to suspect that the pinecone was actually the fruit that Eve ate in the tale of Genesis, that led to Adam and Eve to be expelled from the Garden of Eden and the Fall of Man in Biblical legend. If that is true, than the presence of the Third Eye has had an undeniable impact on civilizations across the globe.

You may be a bit confused on what exactly the Third Eye is. Not to worry -- it's quite hard to conceptualize these aspects of the spiritual world. Simply put, it allows you to see into worlds and states of consciousness that would otherwise be shut off to you. Seeing these things and understanding them is an integral step on the path to enlightenment.

It is referred to by other names, including the inner eye and the eye of knowledge. To utilize your third eye is to have access to not only the inner worlds of yourself, but the higher planes of existence in our universe.

The aim of opening the third eye is the same as most good spiritual healing -- to gain deeper insight into yourself and the world, to 'be more'. You have probably heard that humans currently only use a fraction of their potential contained in their mind. You may have heard of Plato's myth of the cave, in which humans who had lived their whole life in a cave thought that the shadows on the wall were the real world. This remains relevant today. Most people can't begin to think of the wonder that they could see if they allowed themselves to expand their horizons and walk amid the real world, the spiritual world. Instead, they remained trapped in the material world.

In India, the coconut was a potent symbol in a number of rituals it has 'three eyes'. If you look at a coconut, you can see the indentations to which this refers. According to the symbolism, two are 'blind', meaning they don't produce mile when pierced, while the third one is the one you pierce to gain the coconut's milk. In a similar manner, the third eye is the door that you pierce that shows you to the higher planes. This eye gives you the sight to know both yourself and the world around you to a degree that goes most conventional methods of scientific psychological analysis or any method based on interpreting life with your mind grounded in the material world.

Before we get into the procedures to open the third eye, it's important that you have a framework of how you will experience these revelations. It's important to remember to trust your experience. Since there is nothing to believe on the other side of the doors of perception, there is nothing to doubt either! You don't want to take up all your time worrying about whether it is possible that you are really seeing what you are seeing by any objective standards. Trust your experience.

Similarly, when you are in an experience, you don't want to analyze it. Not yet, anyway. You only want to take in the revelations that you are being given. After the experience has finished, you will have plenty of time to break down what happened. Additionally, rational analysis only goes so far when it comes from the third eye. You will receive the most dividends by pondering on your experiences silently and digesting them. By planting the seeds then, your knowledge will mature into a greater understanding of the spiritual world.

So -- I can imagine the question you have. How do I open it? Well, unfortunately, it's not easy. However, it's quite possible for anyone who knows these techniques to do it. It just takes practice, and a willingness to learn from the wisdom of the past.

The truth is that although having the correct methods for expanding your consciousness is important, it's not really style or technique that matters, as far as opening the third eye is concerned. The biggest difference is whether or not you have the capacity to persist along a path. Those who have reached states of great enlightenment have done so because they persisted to the point where there was no earthly obstacle that could stand in their way and the doors to knowledge became clear to them. This kind of dogged persistence is one of the best qualities that you can develop. Even starting from a beginner's level, it is by constant attention to expanding your consciousness that success will come to you.

The first thing that you must do is to become aware of your third eye. It is located in between your eyebrows, above your nose. It can take some time spent on meditation and practice to even reach this step.

To start out, pick a day when you don't have anything planned or other obligations to worry about. The beginning of a weekend or a day you have off work is great. You should plan this initial moment out in advance. After this first time, it will be easier to run through the rest of what you have.

To start out with, remember what you are dealing with is a very subtle sort of perception. What you're feeling won't be anything too dramatic. It could be that you only start out feeling a faint tingling or pressure in the location of your third eye, but that's enough to begin what we're working on. Remember, you want things to come to you.

Some sort of vibration, hard to detect, is already there between the eyebrows in everybody. The purpose of this exercise is to show you how to notice vibration, in order to allow it to blossom into the awakened power of the Third Eye.

Choose a quiet room where you can meditate uninterrupted for at least an hour. You don't have to be alone, but there should not be anyone in the room who is not also participating in the ritual with you. It would be quite counterintuitive for you if you were interrupted by others while you're meditating.

You want to be in a place where you can relax. For guidance on how to achieve this super-relaxed state, see Deep breathing and clearing your mind are great ways to get in the right place to begin exploring the third eye.

To prepare the room, you'll want to light candles around the room. Then comes time to make sure you have the proper attire. You'll want to take off your shoes and undo your belt, tie, or any other articles of clothing you have tied around you, along with your watch.

You'll want to close your eyes; they'll be closed until the end of the exercise. To begin with, you'll want to relax for 2 or 3 minutes. You'll want to be aware of your body and the energy running through it. Focus on that for a while.

Then, after that, you want to just be aware, without any particular concentration on any one part of your body. Allow yourself to embrace the energy.

You now want to be aware of the area between your eyebrows. This is where you'll want to focus your attention, since this is the location of the third eye. Counterintuitively, you don't want to concentrate too much. If you take hold of your Third Eye area with a focus that is too tight, the process can't unfold. Instead, you want to see what happens spontaneously. If your breath starts to become more intense, changing naturally, then you want to follow that and allow that to happen.

You want to remain 'just aware' of this place between your eyebrows, breathing deeply for about 5 minutes. However, it doesn't matter if you have the time exactly right or not, so there's no need to be exactly precise.

Next, place the palm of your hand in front of the area where your third eye chakra is located. Make sure that the hand doesn't touch the skin but hovers above. For a few minutes, stay in this position, lying on the floor with your eyes closed.

Next, you want to put your hand back by your side. Make sure to keep your eyes closed. Then, start looking for a vibration between your eyebrows, as mentioned before. It might feel a number of different ways, either a clear vibration or a sense of tingling. It could even make itself felt as a sense of a rather blurry pressure, a heavy feeling between the eyebrows.

Again, you don't want to try too hard. Remember that it is impossible to force this experience. Take it slow, and wait for this vibration to build up. You want to relax and flow with what comes.

At this point you want to be extremely still. You want to be able to feel the energy around you. It's easier for you to begin to tune into higher states of consciousness when you're still.

This trick here is not focusing too much on your third eye. To achieve this state, you should observe without interaction. It is in this state of passive observation that you will begin to see with your third eye.

Remember, if at any point any of this experience becomes too much for you, you only have to open your eyes again and the session will be over -- you'll instantly be restored to normal consciousness.

You'll have to work at this for a fair amount of time before you start envisioning the sort of sights that you might normally associate with opening the third eye. However, with each meditation session that you attempt to draw out the power of the third eye, you'll gain a deeper and deeper understanding of both yourself and the world around you.

Third Eye Visions

At this point, we'd best clear up some possible misconceptions about sight with the third eye. You aren't seeing visions, as a psychic would. What you are doing instead is expanding your sight into new realms of consciousness. A psychic would feel a type of attachment to the pictures that they see in their consciousness. When reaching visions of Truth, however, you should actually be less interested in the specifics of what you see and focus your attention on the process of opening your mind's eye, allowing your state of consciousness to expand.

When this happens, you come to have an understanding of the higher matters of the universe that is completely different. You'll reach a point where you find that you'll be unable to accurately describe what you have seen because the experience is beyond the tools of language we have for it. Many beginners and folks new to the craft expect to see an exciting new spiritual world with their physical sight and eyes. But this is fundamentally impossible because the part of your mind that processes sight is the part that has been blinded. To see, you must step out of the mind. Again: To see, stop looking. Of course, this will take practice and patience.

One thing to keep in mind is the method by which you will be perceiving things once you open your third eye. This is a bit of a secret among those who already have this knowledge, one that can really change how you approach opening your third eye.

In your everyday life, when you look at something, you look at the different parts of an image, after which what you see is processed by your conscious mind. This is what we normally think of as vision, stemming from the ordinary workings of your mind. However, this mental layer is the part of you that is preventing you from accessing the sight that gives you access to spiritual worlds. In order to become able to see visions of the spiritual world auras and spiritual beings, you have to turn off this mental overlay that is put over vision.

This is the secret that you want to keep in mind; you want to, instead of looking at an image as the sum of its details, focus on the very fact of seeing. Usually, your vision would be occupied by an object in front of you and finding out its particulars, which categories you can assign to the object in your mind. Instead, you want to forget that you should be looking at the components of what you see and instead become aware of the higher concept of seeing. Again, to see, you must stop looking.

Another thing to be aware of when attempting to see with your third eye is the difference in color that you will see. When looking into the higher plan, you won't see light from a sun, or from any sort of lamp. Instead, the objects and beings that you encounter can be seen because they shed their own light. Opening your third eye exposes you to a whole new world of color.

These figures will appear to you as being 'made of colors' in an environment of partial darkness. You should remember, however, that the astral colors a world apart from the physical ones. Again we run into problems with the limitations of our language for describing the mystical experiences. To describe these colors precisely is impossible, due to the lack of counterpoints we can perceive in the material world. For example, you may find that astral colors may appear to you as a mix of different. But when you try to mix the different components of an astral color, it won't seem to work, unlike colors in the material world.

In the material world, you can mix blue and yellow and you'll have green. However, when you open your eyes to the astral world you'll see something different. The colors in the astral world are instead made of many small and very shiny points. As an example, it's possible you'll see a 'blue-yellow-green' in which points of blue, yellow, and green are woven together. This sort of variety and beauty is standard for astral colors, which are rarely uniform. It's impossible to compare these colors to anything that we can observe in our physical reality.

As your third eye begins to develop, it's possible you'll be able to behold more layers of this plan, or even begin to see multiple of these layers at the same time. You may eventually reach a point in the process of opening your third eye where become able to see the physical world and the spiritual world in your vision simultaneously.

This beauty is beyond anything you have experienced. It can actually become too much sometimes, to the point of being unbearable. Your life starts to become a constant wonder, and great fun.

Here is something I recommend you keep in mind as you begin to awaken your third eye; you'll probably find it more satisfying if you don't try to interpret a great deal of the visions you experience. As you go about performing these exercises, you'll see a myriad of wondrous visions. It's best to accept that it will be a while before you can fully comprehend what they mean. To safely interpret the visions you see takes a great deal of experience. Don't let that stop you from trying if you wish though!

Another thing you'll want to keep in mind is which world you are seeing is the real one and which is the "fake" one. Often, when people begin this process of opening the third eye, they usually have preconceptions about what they see. They consider that the physical world, which they experience in their day-to-day lives, is the "real one," and that the non-physical world is only an overlay on reality.

Actually, though, both of these worlds are as real as the other. The only difference is how you perceive them. While you perceive the physical world with your mind, the spiritual world is perceived with your newly discovered third eye.

You may at some point be visited by not just colors or objects but actual beings of the astral plane. These can manifest as spiritual guides for you, or angels, beings of a higher plane. Again, you want to make sure that you don't attempt to force communication with them. As with everything else with the third eye, it's best to first observe and analyze later.

Conclusion

Learning about chakras is a spiritual journey that everyone should take at some point in life. The lessons you learn are useful and will help you change the course of your life. Mastery of your chakras is important in that it accords you an infinite understanding of your spirituality and its connection to the universe around you. What is interesting about chakras is that they are things we know about, but never pay attention to. Most of the time you go about your life like a blind person, unaware of the energy around you, or the energy you emit. Ever wondered why you keep attracting bad company while other people attract good company?

In Sanskrit, you attract similar energy to the one you emit. If you constantly give off negative vibes, you will attract negativity. Those who give off positive energies always have positivity around them. You want nothing but good things in your life. It is time for you to embrace your spirituality, learn about your chakras, and how they affect or control your life. From the first to the last chakra, so much happens in your life that you should learn about. In this book, we covered some of the common symptoms to look for, which will alert you when your chakra is blocked, and what to do. Apart from the emotional and spiritual symptoms, we have also addressed physical experiences that should warn you when something is not right with any of your chakras.

The exercises and routines recommended for balancing your chakras are easy to perform. Allow yourself a few minutes each day for this, and you can get your life back in line. To live and enjoy your life with all the happiness that the universe bestows upon you, the secret lies in a mastery of the seven chakras. Mastery means you understand what they do, and how they control your life.

This level of mastery will help you improve your relationships with people around you, your relationships with nature and the entire universe. Balanced chakras give you peace, not just with people around you, but more importantly, peace with yourself. After all, you cannot know how to love and care for others until you to learn how to do the same for yourself, and the value it holds in your life.

Hopefully, this book will give you a glimpse into a better way of life, and help you overcome most of the challenges that are weighing you down and preventing you from realizing your real potential. Everything you learn about chakra, meditation, your diet, mindfulness, and positivity in this book will help you change the course of your life, and live your best life yet.

CPSIA information can be obtained
at www.ICGtesting.com
Printed in the USA
LVHW050908291120
672813LV00006B/104